Life after God

Life after God

FINDING FAITH WHEN YOU CAN'T BELIEVE ANYMORE

Mark Feldmeir

WESTMINSTER
JOHN KNOX PRESS
LOUISVILLE • KENTUCKY

First edition
Published by Westminster John Knox Press
Louisville, Kentucky

23 24 25 26 27 28 29 30 31 32—10 9 8 7 6 5 4 3 2 1

Book design by Allison Taylor
Cover design by designpointinc.com

Library of Congress Cataloging-in-Publication Data

Names: Feldmeir, Mark, author.
Title: Life after God : finding faith when you can't believe anymore / Mark
   Feldmeir.
Description: First edition. | Louisville, Kentucky : Westminster John Knox
   Press, [2023] | Summary: "Offers an introduction to a God that many
   people weren't aware existed–a mysterious, uncontainable, still-active
   God who loves and cares for real people with real problems"-- Provided
   by publisher.
Identifiers: LCCN 2023013745 (print) | LCCN 2023013746 (ebook) | ISBN
   9780664268404 (paperback) | ISBN 9781646983353 (ebook)
Subjects: LCSH: Faith. | Trust in God--Christianity.
Classification: LCC BV4637 .F37 2023 (print) | LCC BV4637 (ebook) | DDC
   234/.23--dc23/eng/20230530
LC record available at https://lccn.loc.gov/2023013745
LC ebook record available at https://lccn.loc.gov/2023013746

Most Westminster John Knox Press books are available at special quantity discounts when purchased in bulk by corporations, organizations, and special-interest groups. For more information, please e-mail SpecialSales@wjkbooks.com.

To the professor with the loaded finger gun

CONTENTS

Chapter 1

"shh"

the problem of god

You see the beauty of God and you can't say no.

You see the suffering of the world
and you can't stop asking why.

But how do you say yes and dare to ask why
and still call it belief
even as you doubt and
sometimes despair over this beautiful life?
Over this broken world?

You deconstruct.
Then you rebuild.

And what is deconstructing and rebuilding
and rebuilding over and over,
again and again—but an act of faith?

THE DAY OF THE GUN

I'm sitting in a seminary professor's office one afternoon when, all at once, he pulls a gun on me.

He fishes it out of his desk drawer,
points it at my chest, leisurely pulls back the hammer,
and asks me if I believe in God.
It's all so completely unexpected and so seemingly
out of character for a professor who is, by all accounts,

a vegan and
a pacifist and
is known for being really into the universe and
having lots of houseplants and
smoking peyote in the desert and
practicing tai chi and
commuting to campus
on an old Schwinn Wayfarer ten-speed and
wearing a tan corduroy sport jacket
with those brown leather elbow patches.

He is *that* kind of professor.

And he is unquestionably one of the greatest
theological minds of his generation.

And he keeps a loaded handgun in his desk drawer?

The fact that it's a finger gun—imaginary and make-believe—in no way diminishes the gravity of the situation. That I simply do not see any of it coming causes surprising panic. That it comes at the most inconvenient time in my life sparks an immediate crisis of faith.

Because I already know what I believe about God. I don't need to stare down the barrel of a finger gun to find the truth or see the light or test my faith.

I'm 22 years old and

I've been a Christian all my life and
I have experienced what a pastor friend says is a
call to ministry and
I have an undergraduate degree in religious studies,
so I've read Augustine and Aquinas,
Barth and Tillich,
Ruether and Cone and Gutiérrez.

I've even read some Kierkegaard—which is how I know
the gun is ironic.

From behind his cluttered desk, the professor points his
loaded finger gun at me and asks if I believe in God.

What?

A bewildering, disorienting intrusion.

The professor asks me again if I believe in God.

"What? Yes . . ."

The professor then asks me if the God I believe in
is an all-loving God.

"What?"

I hesitate and splutter and tell the professor
that I believe God is love and
it's the nature and character of God to love and
I'd read this somewhere in 1 John and
I remember a theologian referring to this as God's
omnibenevolence.

The professor is unamused by my dubious mastery of
orthodox theological concepts.

He asks me if the God I believe in is an all-powerful God.

And I ask him if by all-powerful he means *omnipotent* as
in, capable of doing anything and limited by nothing and in
control of everything.

And waving his finger gun back and forth, the professor says that by all-powerful he means all of that and also capable of intervening supernaturally in the ordinary events of the natural world which, in my current situation, he says, implies that God has the power to somehow stop the imaginary bullet in his imaginary gun from entering my actual body in the fraction of a second after he pulls the imaginary trigger.

And when I tell the professor that I believe God is omnipotent and has the power to intervene supernaturally in the ordinary events of the natural world, I am suddenly and acutely aware that this entire conversation seems to be unfolding just as the professor had planned.

It's almost like he's done this before—
maybe even dozens of times:
an unsuspecting seminary student,
the prescheduled office hours visit,
the loaded finger gun,
the pointed questions.

He asks me how confident I am, at this moment, that God actually will intervene supernaturally to stop the bullet from entering my chest once he pulls the trigger.

And I confess to him that if this was more than a purely hypothetical situation, that if the gun was real and really loaded, and if the trigger was really pulled, I cannot say that I would be highly confident in God's bullet-intervening supernatural power.

He then reminds me of my earlier assertion—that God is love and all-loving—and asks me how confident I am that God truly desires the absolute best for me.

And I say that I am mostly highly confident that God truly desires the absolute best for me.

And it's here that the professor takes a pause in the

action to summarize for me what seems to be my current
predicament, which is that
the professor has just pulled the trigger,
the bullet has now left the chamber,
God is all-loving and desires the best for me,
God is all-powerful and can intervene supernaturally in
the ordinary events of the world,
and yet the bullet has just entered my chest,
and I am now in quite serious pain,
so how can both statements about God be true?

And I say I do not know because I have just been shot, and
given this highly unanticipated predicament, I'm having
trouble thinking clearly right now and
what exactly is the dilemma?

And the professor returns the finger gun to his desk
drawer and says the dilemma is inherently clear.

If God could have prevented this tragedy but chose not to,
then can we really say with confidence that God is entirely
all-loving and good?

And if God could not have prevented this tragedy,
then can we really say that God is entirely all-powerful?

And because I do not lack for confidence, I believe I know
just enough in this moment to resolve said dilemma.

I tell the professor that this is precisely where free will
comes into play.
God creates us with the capacity for doing and
experiencing both good and evil,
but God can't give us the freedom to do
and experience evil things
and at the same time
prevent us from actually doing or experiencing
evil things because
isn't free will an expression of divine love?

The professor stares at me
with a complete lack of surprise.

He invites me to imagine this scenario:
A toddler is crawling perilously, unwittingly close to the
edge of a sheer cliff and there is nothing to stop the
toddler's tragic fall except for a rock pile hundreds of feet
below.

When the mother and father suddenly spot the toddler
approaching the cliff, the mother jumps to her feet and
attempts to rescue her son before he tumbles over it.

But the father abruptly stops the mother and says,
"I know we could intervene to save our son,
but do we really want to rob him of his free will?"

The professor pauses.

He asks me if I would call that father a loving father,
if it's even possible to call that father a powerful father,
if, in fact, he has imposed limits on his own power to act.

I can see that my free will card isn't playing, so I drop the
next best card in my hand.

I say maybe this whole gun incident is part of God's plan,
that there must be some greater good that will come out
of it, something we cannot see now, from our human,
earthly vantage point.
Maybe what we cannot comprehend today will make
complete sense someday.
Maybe we will eventually see how it all worked for good.
Maybe, given enough time, we will even be strangely
thankful it happened.

The professor informs me that the word for this
theological concept is *omniscience*.
It's the idea that God knows all things—
everything that has ever happened in the past,

everything that is happening right here and now,
and everything that will ever happen in the future.
Yesterday, today, and tomorrow are all
one eternal moment,
already known by God,
already destined by God,
already fulfilled by God.

I tell the professor that maybe this omniscience concept
explains why the Bible says
all things work for good and
everything happens for a reason and
God knows the plans he has for us.

And the professor laughs and says he's trying hard, really
hard, not to pull out that gun from his desk drawer and
shoot me again.

And then he reminds me of my now seriously urgent and
tragically unfolding situation:
I have been shot and
I have a bullet in my chest and
I am bleeding out and
this is not going to end well for me.

He asks me if, in the brief time I still have left in this
earthly life, I'm perhaps starting to question why an
all-loving, all-powerful God would not have chosen to
accomplish his so-called plan
by more loving, less unnecessarily painful
and deadly means.

And I say when you put it that way it does seem a bit
extreme but this is what we call the *mystery* of faith.

It's the last card in my hand. The celebrated *mystery* card
that Christians casually and smugly throw down when
faith and reason become uncomfortably irreconcilable.

The moment I play the mystery card the professor leans in

and asks me if I have a family, and I tell him I have a wife
and a mother and a father and a sister.

He asks me if it would bring comfort to them if,
upon informing them of my untimely death,
he told them this tragedy was all part of God's plan
and everything happens for a reason and
they will just have to accept the mystery of it.

And I tell him please, please, do not ever say that to them
or to anyone.

He asks me what then *should* he say to my family.

And I tell him that maybe first he should tell my family that
he's sorry for shooting me.
And after he says he's sorry for shooting me, he should
not say anything more, because what can you say at a
time like that, and what can you do in a moment like that?

Except cry and
breathe and
hold space and
keep silent?

The professor nods.

Then he announces that regular office hours are over.

THEODICY

Driving home, I try to convince myself that none of what
just transpired in the professor's office was real. The
entire exercise was hypothetical, theoretical, academic.
I cannot make sense of why I'm feeling a deep loss and
strange sadness.

And then I remember a story I had heard about the
seventeenth-century French theologian Blaise Pascal.

But before I tell you *that* story,
there's *another* story about Pascal that maybe you've
heard about—the one about how, early in his life and
career, Pascal proposed that we should analyze the
question of God's existence with a gambler's sense of
logic and calculation.

Pascal argued that belief is a wager: either God exists, or
God does not. Pascal said the odds are essentially 50-50.
So, faced with even odds, and with everything else being
equal, he said we can make our wager based solely on the
potential payout or loss associated with believing.

If we bet that God exists, and we're right,
we stand to gain eternity.
If we bet that God exists, and we're wrong,
we would lose nothing.
If we bet that God does not exist,
and God actually does exist, we might lose eternity.
If we bet that God does not exist, and it turns out
God does not exist, then we gain nothing.

Assuming that mere *belief* in God is the all-determinative
factor in gaining eternity, the gambler's calculation,
motivated purely by payout, compels us to wager that God
exists. We have nothing to lose by believing and being
wrong, but everything to gain by believing and being right.

In Pascal's words, "Reason impels you to believe."[1]

When I first learned about Pascal's wager
in a college philosophy class, I felt genuine sadness over
what Pascal had made of faith, how he'd reduced the
mystery and beauty and revelation of God to
playing the odds and
payouts and losses and
reward and punishment and
reason over belief.

Pascal's faith was devoid of spirit and love
and wonder and joy.
It was reduced to mere probabilities.

Driving home from the professor's office, I feel the same
sadness I felt in that college philosophy class when I
couldn't reconcile Pascal's spirit-barren claim that *reason
impels you to believe.*

Only now, after my encounter with the professor, the
sadness I feel emerges from a new fear that perhaps the
opposite might be true—that *reason actually impedes your
ability to believe.*

The professor had just made the case that God cannot be
both all-loving and all-powerful. A reasonable faith implies
that these two divine attributes are incompatible. At least
one of them must be untrue.

I learned later that theologians refer to this conundrum as
theodicy, from the Greek words *theos*, meaning God, and
dike (pronounced dee-kay), meaning justice. Theodicy
is the rational attempt to justify God's omnipotence
and goodness in view of the existence of evil and the
prevalence of suffering in the world.

Theodicy dares to ask why,
in the midst of suffering,
does God seem absent,
silent, and
even cruel?

This question of theodicy once led C.S. Lewis to write
his well-known book, *The Problem of Pain*, to resolve this
enduring theological puzzle. In it, Lewis wrote famously,
"God whispers to us in our pleasures, speaks in our
conscience, and shouts in our pains: it is His megaphone
to rouse a deaf world."[2]

But later, after the death of his wife, Joy, Lewis

reconsidered his notorious *megaphone theodicy*. In his book *A Grief Observed*, as he pondered whether God might be the "Eternal Vivisector," the "Cosmic Sadist, the spiteful imbecile,"[3] he confessed that, in the end, "you can't see anything properly while your eyes are blurred with tears."[4]

Yale professor and theologian Nicholas Wolterstorff, following the death of his son, Eric, in a mountain-climbing accident at the age of 25, came to see theodicy not as an intellectual puzzle to solve but as an unwelcome, insoluble invasion to endure. "I do not know why God would watch [Eric] fall," he wrote candidly. "I do not know why God would watch me wounded. I cannot even guess."[5]

In the Hebrew Bible, the book of Job is considered a work of theodicy. Job personifies our universal struggle to believe in God in the face of indefensible suffering and loss. Shaking his fist at God, he dares to ask what no one wants to ask, but everyone will likely ask some day,

> (W)hat do I do to you, you watcher of humanity?
> Why have you made me your target?
> Why have I become a burden to you?[6]

For so many people, personal faith is often maimed or killed at the intersection of divine goodness and human suffering.

JENGA

Driving home, it feels as if that one Jenga block that's been holding up the entire tower of my faith system has now become irreversibly vulnerable, precarious, dubious.

What happens when you pull what seems irrational, like divine omnipotence, from the puzzle of faith?

The tower begins to wobble, sway, lean to one side.

That's when I remember this *other* story about Pascal
and how, at the age of 31, he experienced a
strange mystical vision of the divine
that compelled him to abandon the world of reason and,
as he said, "to live for God alone."

He died eight years later, having never told anyone about
that transformative mystical experience.

But on the night it happened, he abruptly rejected reason
as a basis for faith. He forsook his notorious gambler's
logic and calculation in pursuit of a complete return to the
Bible and divine revelation.

When Pascal died, his servant found sewn into his jacket
a brief document titled "Memorial," which summarized his
mystical experience and included the words—
"God of Abraham, God of Isaac, God of Jacob, not of the
philosophers and scholars.... Forgetfulness of the world
and of everything, except God."[7]

Driving home, I remember that story and the sadness
begins to subside, and my wobbling Jenga-like block tower
of faith starts to straighten and settle again.

Forget the professor's reason and logic,
the philosophers and scholars,
the make-believe gun,
the imaginary bullet in my chest,
the glaring contradictions of my faith,
the sad conversation with my family about a tragedy that
never happened.

Forget the world and everything, except God.

But then I go to work the following morning. And I have no
choice but to remember the world.

WHAT'S REAL AND WHAT ISN'T

To make ends meet while in seminary, I worked as a
phlebotomist at a county hospital, drawing blood
from the arms of the poor and the indigent who do
not have the luxury of forgetting about the world and
everything except God.

Some are gang members with real bullets lodged in
their brains and armed deputies guarding their rooms and
bereft mothers praying the rosary by the bedsides of their
comatose teenage sons.

Some are gay men and IV drug users secreted away
in half-lit isolation rooms, suffering from a mysterious,
leprous, fatal disease for which there is no cure, only
shame and stigma and death.

Some are heroin addicts with track marks so scarred and
calloused that my needle bends as I forage and fish futilely
for a viable vein.

Some are innocent children who wandered too close to
that sheer cliff the professor spoke about and tumbled
over the edge and landed among the world's rock piles,
suffering unimaginable tragedy and irrecoverable loss.

From the desperate moans of the burn unit to the shrieks
of the incarceration ward, from the chaos of the ER to the
quiet vigils on the ICU, I keep coming back to the questions
sparked by that conversation in the professor's office.

How can one speak of an all-loving, all-powerful God
amid such immeasurable suffering and human wreckage?

What can be said of God in this godforsaken place
that will not offend the tender souls of the suffering?

How, here, can one forget the world and everything,
except God?

Is it ever possible to say yes and dare to ask why
and still call it belief
even as you doubt and sometimes despair
over this beautiful life?
Over this broken world?

Within days of my conversation with the professor, my
48-year-old father is diagnosed with terminal cancer.

Then, weeks later, a close friend, whose baby is due to be
born the same week as ours, calls with the devastating
news that his daughter has just been delivered stillborn.

Then, over the subsequent months,
a hospital coworker is killed in a head-on collision and
my best friend's sister is sexually assaulted and
American troops are invading Iraq and
Kurt Cobain swore he didn't have a gun
but it turns out he did and
a hurricane kills 65 people in Florida and
four LAPD officers are acquitted for beating
Rodney King and
the City of Los Angeles is burning.

And my father is dying.

And that's when I can see what is real and what isn't real.

In the real world
the gun is real and
the bullet is real and
the questions are real and
the glaring contradictions of our faith are real and
the inexplicable evil and suffering in the world is real.

How can the world and everything except God be
forgotten?

And what isn't real
is the only God I have ever known—

the all-powerful, all-knowing, changeless,
and timeless God
that sometimes seemingly
does not care or
does not intervene or
does not understand or
does not feel.

Or does not exist.

WHO SAID THAT?

My faith meant everything until it didn't, and suddenly I'm
afraid and even ashamed of what that means, because
I'm studying to be a pastor and everything in my life has
been leading to this *calling*.

And who, by the way, goes to seminary
and loses their faith?

That's when I remember that line from Samuel Beckett,
"You must go on. I can't go on. I will go on."

And I tell myself that I want to believe,
that I still believe,
that I don't know what I believe.
But I will try to believe.

And that's when I hear someone or something say, *Shh!*

I don't know exactly who or what said it,
or where it even came from.
But it stabbed.
It shamed.
It silenced.

It may have been my own conscience. It may have been
the church, or a preacher, a friend or mentor, or someone

who knew and loved and depended on me. It may have been my imagined future.

But it wasn't my imagination.

"Shh!"

What? Why, *Shh?*

Because we don't talk about these things.

I tell you all of this because chances are the *Shh!*
is as real for you as it was for me, and
because there is for all of us
the gun
and the bullet
and the questions
and the contradictions
and the faint sound of your own voice whispering,
"I want to believe
but I don't know what I believe or
how to believe."

Maybe you see the beauty of God and you can't say no,
but you see the suffering of the world and you can't stop
asking why.

Maybe you believe and doubt and despair
and you want to know that even this is faith.

But then someone, something,
some collective voice says, *Shh!*
And then you stop asking why.
And then you stop saying yes.
And then you just stop believing.

But what is deconstructing and rebuilding
and rebuilding over,
again and again,
but an act of faith?

THE ELEPHANT IN THE ROOM

There's a *New Yorker*-type cartoon that depicts a group of people sitting politely on couches in a small room, all staring blankly at each other, pretending to ignore the massive elephant sitting in the lap of one of them, whose name we're about to learn is Alan.

The giant pachyderm is crushing Alan, but no one in the room is doing anything about it.

Below, the caption reads: "Only Alan was prepared to acknowledge the elephant in the room."

There's a glaring truth sitting elephant-like in the hearts of a growing number of people today.

Perhaps it sits in your heart.

No one wants to talk about it, but we all know it's there.

It's an uncomfortable truth. Pollsters have surveyed it. Experts have written volumes about it. Empty pews in so many churches have confirmed it. And more and more of us are finally naming it.

This elephant-in-the-room,
unsettling truth
is that we have a God problem in the modern world.
It's not a problem with *God*
so much as it's a problem with what Christianity has made of God,
how Christianity has conceived of God,
and the claims that Christians have made about God.

This God problem is not one of experience but of perception. More and more people are actively pursuing spiritual experiences and holy encounters that cultivate joy, meaning, purpose, and beauty in their lives. They're giving more attention to their spirituality and to spiritual practices than ever before.

They're just not doing it within the conventional structures of organized Christianity.

Twenty-seven percent of U.S. adults (one in four) now say they think of themselves as "spiritual but not religious," up 8 percentage points in five years.[8]

By contrast, 63 percent (two in three) of U.S. adults self-identify as Christians, down from 75 percent (three in four) a decade ago.[9]

Maybe you're one of the growing number of people who identify as *spiritual but not religious*—the *SBNRs*, as demographers have come to call them.
Maybe you're not so much living life *without* God, but living life *after* the God you can no longer believe in.

Many so-called SBNRs can no longer reconcile the all-loving, all-powerful, all-knowing God they've been told about and taught about with their real, lived experience of God in the world. Their doubts, questions, and suspicions had been silenced and condemned for so long that the elephant in the room just kept getting bigger and heavier and more harmful to them.

Until finally, they simply chose to leave the room to pursue life after God.

But imagine if,
instead of silently watching them leave the room,
we were brave enough to evict the elephant.

Imagine if, without the elephant,
we suddenly found the real God who's been with us all along—
a God who is found in the ancient stories of the Bible, yet whom we have largely ignored in favor of another.

Only when we can dare to live life after a God we can no longer believe in can we be freed to live life in pursuit of a God we were never told about—

a God who persuades out of love
rather than coerces out of power,
who feels what we feel and responds accordingly,
who is both unchanging yet ever-changing, and
who is too busy offering new possibilities
in the unfolding present
to confine our futures to a predetermined plan.

What if the real God of the Bible is working for us
and with us,
experiencing and responding to us,
wooing us and waiting for us
on the other side of life after the only God
we've ever known?

DON'T SHUSH ME

The Biosphere 2 project is an American Earth system
science research facility located in Oracle, Arizona. It was
created to serve as a center for research and teaching
about Earth's living systems and its place in the universe.
It's an artificial, materially closed ecological system—
otherwise known as a *vivarium*. It remains the largest
closed ecological system ever created.

But one of the most profound discoveries made by the
scientists had nothing to do with a cure for some new
disease or innovative methods of farming and ecology.

Instead, the discovery had to do with the role of wind
in the lives of trees.

The trees inside Biosphere 2 grew rapidly—
more rapidly than they did outside of the dome.

But they also fell over before reaching maturation.

After examining the root systems and outer layers of
their bark, scientists came to realize that a lack of wind

in Biosphere 2 caused a deficiency of stress wood.
Stress wood helps a tree position itself for optimal sun
absorption; it also helps trees grow more solidly.
Without stress wood, a tree can grow quickly,
but it cannot support itself fully. It cannot withstand
normal wear and tear and survive.

Trees need some resistance to thrive over time.

So it is with faith.

Doubts, questions, resistance, finger guns and hard
conversations, and county hospitals are vital to the soul.
Without them, the roots of our faith run shallow.
We stumble and tumble over.

There's an ancient story about a man named Jacob
who has this extraordinary dream. In the dream Jacob is
given to see that his whole life has meaning and purpose
beyond what he had previously imagined.

Before the dream, he wonders, like all of us:
Where did we come from?
How did we get here?
What are we doing here?
Where are we going?
How are we getting there?

In the dream, Jacob sees that he's a part of something
bigger than his own story—and yet his own story is
indispensable to the ways in which God's bigger, more
expansive story will ultimately unfold. Jacob's life has a
purpose within some larger purpose.

When he awakens from the dream, he says, "Surely the
LORD is in this place—and I did not know it!"[10]

The Jewish sages taught that Jacob's story suggests
there's another world—a dimension of the spiritual—right
here within this world, that lies open to us whenever we
awaken to it and pay attention to it. Like Joseph, we can

access that world from this world, if only we can learn to see differently.

Sometimes we need a changed perception to discover
that God has been here all along.
Sometimes we need to awaken to
a whole new awareness of
who God is
and where God is
and how God relates to us
and why we are here
and where all of this is going.

Jacob's story reminds us that we don't have to
leave the room to wake up.

We only have to evict the elephant that shames and
denies and silences our very real, lived experience—the
elephant that says, *Shh!*

Only then can we keep saying yes
to the beauty of God and
keep asking our whys to the suffering of the world and
keep daring still to call that faith and
keep saying to the elephant,
"Don't shush me."

Chapter 2

"psst"

the call of god

I was watching one of those TV shows where they roll home videos of people doing ill-advised things that should have killed them but didn't.

It's like *America's Funniest Videos*.
Only without the laugh track.

If your idea of entertainment is watching people bungee jump from tall bridges only to discover half-way down that they failed to secure the other end of the rope to the bridge, then you would for sure really enjoy this show.

In the episode I was watching, a group of college-aged women board a small drift boat on a river somewhere in the Midwest. They're enjoying a quiet, leisurely afternoon on the water when, all at once, the sky above turns ominously greenish black; tornado-like winds descend upon the halcyon river carrying thunderheads that, without warning, unleash an apocalyptic downpour of rain and hail and chaos.

Within minutes, the river rises and swells and rushes with storm surge and whitecaps and muddy swill. Everyone on the river is scrambling for cover. But as these five women collect themselves and prepare to head for the dock, they soon discover that, with the river's current now erupting, the motor on their little boat isn't strong enough to get them back upstream to safety.

In no time, they're drifting steadily downstream toward a ten-foot-high dam—which presents the viewer with the highly anticipated *now-wait-for-it* moment of the episode.

Inevitably, as the boat finally reaches the dam, it topples over the edge, landing at the base of the dam—still somehow upright, but strangely, impossibly stuck in the whirlpool-like current of the waterfall.

Surprisingly, all five women are still safely inside the boat.

But the force of the current will not release the boat.

The boat is taking on water.

This is when the narrator says, in typical dramatic fashion, "Of the five women in the boat, one of them cannot swim."

Isn't this why we watch? Someone with a video camera has chosen to film this unfolding calamity instead of intervening—precisely because we watch.

As the boat continues to take on water, it finally capsizes, spilling all five women into the raging river.

Chaos ensues.

The four swimmer-types let go of the side of the boat and swim to the rescue boats that are now waiting for them downstream. But the non-swimmer-type stays with the capsized boat, clinging to its hull in desperation. She will not leave the boat, even as she struggles to hold on.

She slips under the surface of the water.
She comes back up.
She slips back under again.
Over and over.

The narrator reveals the obvious.
She will drown if she refuses to let go
of that hopeless boat.
She holds on to save herself,
but her only chance of survival is to let go and surrender herself to the raging waters.

The drama goes on and on. She disappears below the surface, then comes back up, gasping for air, again and again.

Why do we watch?

We watch because we feel. We watch because we sense that somehow, somewhere, it is us, or will be us, holding out for hope, holding on to nothing, holding our breath, grasping and gasping for air.

The rescuers call to her from downstream.

"You can do this."

Over and over, they call, plead, coax.

"You can do this."

Until she can resist their calls no longer.

Too exhausted to hold on,
too weak to continue fighting the current,
she comes to her senses.
Clinging to a sinking boat is futile.
She must trust that her rescuers waiting downstream will not let her drown.

That's when the moment of surrender at last arrives.
She lets go of the boat.
She is carried downriver like spindly driftwood
buoyed up by some inexplicable grace
until the outstretched arms of strangers find her
and she is drawn from the raging river
like one raised to life from the waters of baptism.

WE'RE ALL IN THE SAME STORM

One of the earliest and most enduring symbols of the
Christian church is that of a small wooden boat sailing on
the stormy seas. You can find images of boats displayed in
stained glass windows in many modern churches, carved
in sculptures from the Renaissance era, and etched in
iconography from the days of the early church.

In ancient times,
the sea was the symbol of terror and death and chaos,
the only part of creation that hadn't been tamed by God,
where the enemy of goodness lurked,
where the forces of evil skulked.

In an age when everyone seemed to believe in
leviathan and sea monsters
and an earth so flat you could sail straight off the edge,
leaving the shoreline for open waters
in a rickety wooden boat
required great courage and faith.

The symbol of the boat, for early Christians, was
reminiscent of the stories found in the Gospels in which
Jesus and his disciples sailed the Sea of Galilee. From a
small wooden boat, Jesus calmed the storms, silenced
the wind and the waves, walked on water, and taught his
followers to trust.

Over the centuries, the church adopted the spiritual

symbolism of the boat to establish itself as the essential vessel of salvation in the world. In a dangerous, turbulent, unpredictable world in which evil always seems to lurk just beneath the surface, the boat—the church—was believed to be our only refuge.

This is why, in church architecture, the central portion of cathedrals and church sanctuaries is called the *nave*. The Latin for ship is *navis*, and for boat, or small ship, it's *navicula*.

The church, the community of believers and all the orthodox traditions, creeds, doctrines, and beliefs—taken together—have always been understood as something like an imperiled little boat tossed on the vast and swirling sea of unbelief and disbelief, of worldliness and relativism, of persecution and hardship.

The church claimed that only by divine providence and steadfast faith can that boat reach safe harbor with its treasured cargo of human souls.

But for many moderns, that boat is caught
in the mounting whirlpool of
hypocrisy
irrelevance
archaic thinking
judgmentalism
certitude
dogmatism
scandal
silence
complicity
anti-science.

Most would agree that the boat is taking on water.
Many suspect that the boat has already capsized.
More and more are convinced that the boat is simply too small and too confining,

that there's not enough room in the boat for questions,
for doubts,
for doubters and skeptics.
And a growing number are struggling to
remain in the boat, to believe—
if believing means having to accept all the things
they've been told about God
that are no longer buoyant and believable.

For them, it feels far safer to leave the boat behind.
To live life after God.

Have you ever felt like that woman caught in the endless
whirlpool, clinging to the side of a hopeless boat,
drowning—yet still afraid of what it might mean if you
were to let go?

I went to seminary to become a pastor and I lost my faith.
It's not supposed to happen that way, but it happened.
I came face-to-face with the real possibility that I didn't
know what I believed, or if I believed, or how I could ever
believe.

A lot of people have serious doubts and questions about
their faith and the boat they've chosen. But in my case,
those doubts and questions came at the very worst time.
I was studying to be a pastor. I was about to be ordained.

My whole life up until then seemed to have been moving
toward this singular purpose, this *call to ministry*, to which
I had said yes with alacrity. I was leading Bible studies
and youth retreats in my church. I had people in my life—
family members, mentors, pastors, teachers—who were all
cheering me on. And I had this idealistic, high-achieving,
hypercritical Holden Caulfield-type conscience with a
highly tuned phony detector that demanded I live and act
with integrity of belief.

It was a massive, messy, mangled, tangled hairball of
God-consciousness and

divine calling and
naiveté and
self-confidence and
perfectionism and
certainty and
fear and
self-doubt and
dread.

My crisis of faith came like a sudden downpour.
The raging river of doubt, the relentless stream of
questions, swirled and swelled all around me.
My little boat quickly started taking on water, and when it
finally capsized, I held on to the side of that boat until
I couldn't hold on any longer, until I realized that holding
on would mean losing something vital to my soul.
So, I did the only thing I could do.

I let go of the boat.

I plunged headfirst into all my doubts and questions.

I swam all the way to the bottom of the river. I discovered
how deep and scary and lonely and beautiful and quiet
and liberating it was all at once.

I held my breath under the water for as long as I could,
for months, for years, for too long, until I could
no longer hear the *Shh!* that stabs and silences and
shames the doubter.

I held my breath until I heard the most irresistible and
evocative voice calling me back to the surface and
allowing me to breathe again.

All it said was *Psst!*

I didn't know where it came from, but it felt like release,
rescue, redemption.

I didn't know what it meant, but it sounded like:

you can do this,
you can be this!

Eventually, I dared to resurface with a more compelling
reason to believe, and a more honest and convincing
reason to become a pastor: to build a bigger and more
buoyant boat—a lifeboat—for people who struggle with
doubts and questions but still bravely wonder if there
might be a God they haven't yet met. A God they can
honestly believe in.

HELP MY UNBELIEF

Some of the most poignant and courageous conversations
I've since had as a pastor are with those who,
for any number of reasons, can simply no longer
believe in the God they've been told about or taught about
over the years.

These conversations are invariably hard. But they are
most often spoken in extraordinary honesty and humility.
Somewhere deep within them I can hear something of
my own life-long struggle to believe all the irreconcilable
things I always assumed I had to believe to elude the label
of doubter or skeptic or heretic.

People will confess to me, often with some degree of
guilt or anguish, and usually in a hushed whisper, as if
disclosing a terrible secret that must never be openly
shared:

> "At this point in my life, I don't know *what* I believe
> anymore."
> "After [fill in the blank] happened to me, I don't know
> *how* I can believe anymore."
> "Given what I now know about how the world really
> works, I don't know *if* I believe anymore."

Perhaps you're one of them. Perhaps you've struggled with faith, or what organized Christianity has made of faith, and you've chosen to live life after God—a kind of post-God, or post-Christian life.

Over the centuries, Christianity has been plagued by binary thinking that suggests you can't be a Christian unless you believe a certain way and unless you're certain about what you believe.

This binary thinking leaves little or no room for
questions,
uncertainty,
doubt,
and the inevitable
but-what-if or
I-don't-know moments.

It has created a wake of spiritual trauma for a growing number of would-be believers, and it's the catalyst behind the emergent swell of spiritual refugees fleeing the boat and freeing themselves of Christianity in pursuit of a post-God life.

If you're not certain whether you believe
or what you believe or
whether you even can believe,
you are not alone.

When it comes to belief in God, we're experiencing a major sea change in the US:

Over the last 60 years, belief in God has been consistently trending downward. By 2070, it's projected that fewer than 50 percent of Americans will identify as Christian.[1]

Eighty-one percent (about four out of five) of Americans today say they believe in God. This is down 6 percentage points over the last five years, 11 points over the last decade, and 17 points over the last six decades.

This decline in belief is driven primarily by young adults and those who identify as "liberals." Today, only 68 percent of young adults, and 62 percent of those on the left of the political spectrum, believe in God.

But even among those who *do* report belief in God, there's not much consensus about what we're even talking about when we talk about God and how God works in our lives or in the world. For example, about half of those who believe in God (42 percent of all Americans) say God hears prayers and can intervene on a person's behalf. Meanwhile, 28 percent of all Americans say God hears prayers but cannot intervene. And 11 percent of all Americans say God doesn't hear prayers or intervene at all.[2]

There's no doubt we have a belief problem.
But could it be that, at the heart of our belief problem, is a crisis of understanding?

Could it be that our traditional understanding of the God of the Bible has created a conception of God that many simply cannot reconcile with their lived experience?

Could it be that it's not actually God, but our interpretation of the Bible, that's no longer believable?

In his famous *Leaves of Grass*, the great poet Walt Whitman once gave some extremely impractical advice. He said, "Re-examine all you have been told at school or church or in any book, dismiss whatever insults your own soul, and your very flesh shall be a great poem."

But before you dismiss everything or even anything you already believe, attend first to that which you know, through your lived experience, has gladdened your soul and added beauty and wonder and joy to your life. Consider the very real possibility that such experiences might be

hints of the transcendent,
holy epiphanies,
divine encounters,
the quiet, hidden work of God.
Behold them with kindness and reverence and
astonishment. Protect them fiercely, even if they do not
conform to what tradition or convention or orthodoxy
calls authoritative or even real. Love them for what
they are, for their courage to have shown up, for their
companionship, for their generosity. Hold them closely,
tenderly. Give thanks.

Then, consider all that which simply does not add up
or stack up or measure up to your lived experience,
and hold these delicately, too—
the questions and doubts and
the myths and stories and
the rituals and practices and traditions and
the creeds and doctrines and even the dogmas and
all the things about God that you've been taught but never
understood or believed.

Before you dismiss or discard any of these, give
them permission to exist, to sit beside you, to just be.
Sometimes we need to live alongside the tension of what
we do not believe to finally and fully embrace what we
might believe. Sometimes what we never could believe
or even what we cannot believe today will, given enough
time, become something like a friend or mentor or muse
or generous antagonist that stretches and challenges and
keeps us from getting too cozy or complacent with what
we are comfortably willing to believe now.

But if, while sitting beside you, any of these happen to
get too noisy or needy or accusatory or manipulative or
judge-y or shame-y—or, worse, if they start to show their
teeth or become aggressive or intrusive or hurtful to the

point of *insulting your soul,* carefully pick up
each of them by the tail, one at a time.
Casually listen to them scream and whine helplessly.
Remain calm. Tell them thanks for sharing,
but it's time for them to move on now.
Take one last look at them for what they are
and what they can no longer be for you or do to you.

Then, one by one, take them to the nearest doorway
that leads from your heart to the outside world,
and let them go. Set them free. If at first they refuse
to leave on their own, call for the dogs, reach for a shoe,
turn the hose on them. Do whatever is necessary
to make them go away.

Watch them scamper off. Love them for what they
used to be or might have been. Say a prayer.
Breathe deeply. Give thanks.

And then close the door and return to your self—to that
part of your soul that's been held hostage for far too
long—and consider how, after all the brave work you've
just done, your very flesh might finally be free enough to
become more like a great poem and less like a tortured
lament.

Because only then are we able to comprehend how doubt
can become the purest form of belief,
and disbelief can become the surest path to salvation,
and life after God can become the most honest and
beautiful expression
of life in pursuit of a God who has been here all along.

Only then will you be able to hear the *Psst!* of God over the
Shh! of the world.

And the *Psst!* is everywhere.

Can you hear the *Psst!* of God?

WOO ME

One aspect of faith that moderns seem most uncertain about is how God works in their lives and in the world.

Does God get involved in the ordinary events and affairs of human life and the natural world? Does God work *supernaturally*—intervening in everyday affairs, in real time, as they're unfolding, to achieve some divine purpose?

Most of us might truly hope so. The events of the world can feel so random. We can feel so helpless. We want to believe that God is in charge.

Sometimes we can look back over the course of our lives, at the inexplicable events of our past, and sense that, all along, there was something, some presence or force or higher power, working behind the scenes on our behalf.

We begin to connect the dots of everything that has ever happened over the course of our lives—the moments of ache and the glimpses of awe,
the hard-won victories and the magnificent defeats,
the terrible things we've endured and
the seemingly random and senseless things we didn't at the time understand—
and maybe we can see a pattern emerging,
a story that suggests both a guiding presence and
a unique purpose to our lives.

I have a friend who should have been at his desk in Tower 2 when the planes struck the World Trade Center on September 11. But just as he was leaving his apartment that morning, he chose to take an unexpected phone call from his mother. That phone call made him just late enough to miss his regular morning train.

He never made it to his desk that morning. Those that did never made it back home that evening.

What do you call that?

Some might call it the hand of God, but the families of those who didn't come home that day certainly would not.

I remind myself of this as I'm sitting with a mother who, the day after her 16-year-old son is killed in a roll-over car accident, comes to my office seeking answers to how or why God would ever allow her boy to die.

Or as I'm visiting a man in county jail who is so crippled by addiction that he's lost nearly everything meaningful in his life; who, speaking through a phone from behind a thick panel of plexiglass, asks me, "Why will God not take this affliction from me?"

Or when I hear an Alabama senator on the evening news, a day after Hurricane Katrina strikes the Gulf Coast, claiming the storm hit where it did because Mississippi and Louisiana have legalized gambling. "God sent the hurricane to punish those states for their sin," he prophesizes—which curiously fails to explain why Katrina destroyed only eight casinos but hundreds of churches.

How does God work? What can we say that won't insult the soul?

Maybe the most reliable clue we have about how God works is found in what the Bible describes as God's very first act in the world—that first moment before human time when the world as we know it came into being.

Consider the very first verse of the first chapter of the first book of the Bible. In this ancient creation poem, God's spirit sweeps like a bird over a soupy mess of chaos, a bottomless swirl of emptiness, an inky splotch of churning, swirling space dust.[3]

In the Hebrew, all this preexistent, primordial chaos and disorder is called *tohu va-vohu*—the wild and waste, the empty and void between being and not-being.

God sees within all that *tohu va-vohu* some hidden
potential and possibility for life, beauty, order.

God's spirit swoops over it, sees it, and cannot resist it
or remain silent in the face of it.

And so God speaks to it. God issues an invitation to it,
beckoning to it: "Let there be ..."

God coaxes and summons
the sun,
the moon,
the stars,
the oceans and dry land,
the grasses and trees and shrubs,
the caddis fly and long-horned beetle and cutthroat trout
and golden eagle and great bison
into becoming, order, diversity, abundance, and goodness.

It is God's first recorded act in time and space.
God's first move comes in the form of a flirtatious,
luring call: "Let there be ..."

And this is really odd, by the way.

Why doesn't God simply gaze into the *tohu va-vohu*
and utter a straightforward command—
like a film director might declare on a Hollywood set,
"Lights, camera, action!"

Why are God's first words, *"Let there be ..."*?

Linguists tell us this strange *"let there be"* phrase appears
in what's called the "jussive" mood of the verb "to be."
The jussive mood is a rare verb form.
While it's a form of a command, it's not like the more
common imperative form of a command in which the
one speaking might compel or coerce a subject to do
something—like a mother telling her child to put on her
shoes, or your jerky dictator boss demanding that you
complete that big project by Friday's deadline.

The jussive mood is different.
It's not coercive.
It's simply a form of hopeful expression that something
could happen,
might happen,
will happen.

But it doesn't have to happen.
It might not happen.

The call is nothing more than the speaker's deepest desire
that it will happen—
a wish,
a hope,
a dream.

At Christmas, when Frank Sinatra sings, "Let it snow,
let it snow, let it snow," the singing doesn't make it snow.
It only expresses his dreamy blue-eyed desire
to see the snow fall.

God's first creative deed is an act of dreaming out loud,
a spoken wish for the *tohu va-vohu* that swirls and stirs
prior to creation to come to light and life.

God's very first words, "Let there be," sweep over the *tohu
va-vohu* stuff, permeating it, animating it, with the divine
desire to live.

First things can tell us a lot about someone.

And God's very first interaction with the universe is
completely absent of coercion.

Here, in the opening scene of the ancient creation story,
there is only persuasion—
You can do this.
You could be this.

This is our first reliable clue about how God works
in our lives and in our world.

God will not,
God does not,
God cannot
force anything
or anyone
to do anything
at any time.

Instead, God calls, beckons, lures, and persuades the
chaos toward action and order and life and beauty.

Our traditional ways of understanding God cannot
rationally and coherently explain
how a phone call would make a friend
late to work on 9/11 or
why a man would relapse over and over again or
why a car accident would take a mother's teenage son.
Such events suggest there's something other than God at
work in the world—something *tohu va-vohu*—that has the
power to respond or to resist the call of God.

The God of the Bible is a God whose power is expressed
not in the capacity to make something happen, to prevent
something from happening, or to coerce anything or
anyone to act, but in the power to persuade us to pursue
the divine wish, dream, hope that the *tohu va-vohu* stuff
of our lives and world would say yes to all the hidden
possibility that only God can fully perceive.

Some theologians call this divine power of persuasion the
lure of God[4] that draws, leads, entices, and calls us and all
creation forward by saying,

Psst!
You can do this!
You could be this!

But the choice to respond, to pursue, to follow the dream
is always ours.
The *tohu va-vohu* can resist the lure.

Creation can ignore the invitation.
We can at any moment say no to the divine dream.

The ancient rabbis taught that the creation of the universe is never finished. From the very beginning, the universe was created in an ongoing, uncompleted state, and it only exists by continually saying yes to the call of God. If, at any moment, creation altogether says no, the universe would return to primeval chaos and disorder—back to *tohu va-vohu*.

God lures.
We respond and pursue and
become more than we are.

This collaborative, co-creating relationship is
how we got here,
how we remain here, and
how we live and move and have our being
while we still *are* here.

BECKONED BY BEAUTY

Some Christians are uncomfortable with the metaphor of "the lure." Perhaps it conjures up images of creepy men driving white vans through the neighborhood, or connotes the so-called carnal powers of immorality, temptation, sin. The popular assumption is that what lures us is somehow artificial, not real, and not of God.

But love is real. Wonder, beauty, awe, hope—
these are real.

Have you ever been lured, persuaded,
beckoned by beauty or love?

I awakened to the most breathtaking sunrise recently.
A Colorado sunrise along the Front Range is incomparable.

On this particular morning, the entire sky was awash in flaming hues of red and orange and yellow.

I took a chance and shook Lori from her sleep.

"Come and watch this sunrise," I said.
"It's like God is showing off."

I coaxed her out of bed, ushered her to the window, and we both looked on in quiet wonder and awe, speechless and thunderstruck.

Beauty beckons. Love lures.
Meaning calls out to us every day.

What gets you out of bed every day?

A friend once told me that the Japanese have a word for what gets us out of bed. As a young child, he, his family, and more than 10,000 other Japanese Americans were incarcerated at the Granada Relocation Center in southeastern Colorado during World War II. Forcibly exiled from their communities, grieving the loss of home and livelihood and the rhythms and routines of their daily lives, they suddenly found themselves living in cramped Army-style barracks, surrounded by barbed wire fencing and tall watchtowers manned around the clock by armed guards.

To combat their grief and hopelessness, the internees had to find a reason to get out of bed every morning, so they took to farming the 9,000 acres of the compound, growing a variety of crops and raising livestock.
The Japanese, he told me, call this reason for living *ikigai*. Our ikigai is that sense we have when we wake up that today is not trivial, that it matters, that there are new experiences waiting for us, that beauty and meaning are hanging out on our doorstep, hoping to meet us and beckon us out of the house and into the world to make some important contribution that only we can make.

Our ikigai is our reason for being. It gets us out of bed every day. It lures us to what is beautiful and lovely and meaningful and wonderful.

It says, *Psst!*

POWER TO THE PEOPLE

There are two kinds of power that humans are most apt to wield in the world.[5]

The first, *unilateral power*, is the ability to produce
intended or desired effects in our relationships
through influence, manipulation, or control
to advance our purposes.
Unilateral power is
one-sided,
one-directional,
one-dimensional,
non-relational in nature,
and almost always diminishes or robs the agency
of the other.

It takes whatever is necessary to get whatever it wants.

Unilateral power is the kind of power wielded by
bullies who steal lunch money on the school playground,
tyrants and dictators who bend or break the rules
to cling to power,
and narcissistic leaders in families, corporations,
institutions, organizations, and churches who abuse
their positions for self-gain.

Unilateral power, as the familiar proverb says,
is the kind of *absolute power that corrupts absolutely*.

And it's the kind of power many people today most often associate with God.

The second kind of power, *relational power*,
is the capacity both to influence the other
and to be influenced by the other.

Relational power is grounded in
mutuality,
openness,
responsiveness,
persuasion,
and interdependence.

It involves both giving and receiving.

Relational power desires and works for the highest good
for the other without forcing or imposing one's own needs,
feelings, conditions, or values on the other for achieving
that highest good. As such, relational power voluntarily
places self-limits on one's own needs and ideals, always
acting in ways that honor and preserve the other's
self-identity, freedom, and agency.

Consequently, relational power necessarily involves
being influenced or affected by the other, feeling and
receiving the experience of the other, without losing
one's own self-identity, agency, and essence.

Relational power is the kind of power we long for.

It's the kind of power parents might exercise when
they teach their child how to ride a bike or cross the
street; or when, with bittersweet tears, they drop off
their eighteen-year-old at college, knowing both the risks
and rewards that come with letting go.

It's the kind of power a teacher might exercise
when sacrificing personal time to help a struggling
student so full of promise.

It's the kind of power shared whenever anyone chooses to
suffer or to leverage their privilege for the sake of another,
or for the common good, or for some greater purpose.

Relational power is the kind of power expressed in the timeless covenant between God and Israel, which the ancient rabbis taught was akin to a marriage between two lovers, opening both God and the people equally to genuine vulnerability and the possibility of suffering, disappointment, fulfillment, and enjoyment.

And relational power is the kind of power Jesus embodied in his earthly ministry, always luring, persuading, calling, and, ultimately, suffering for others.

One verb that perhaps best describes the nature and mission of Jesus' Galilean ministry is the Greek word, *kaleo*. It means *to call, to invite,* or *to summon.* It occurs more than 100 times in the New Testament, portraying Jesus as the Divine Wooer who
calls strangers to come and follow,
lures the lame to walk,
beckons the blind to see,
coaxes the dead from their tombs,
persuades outcasts to leave their shadows,
summons religious elites from their bunkers
of piety and pretense,
woos doubters to new ways of believing.

Relational power is persuasion toward possibility.

Psst!
You can do this!
You could be this!

THE GOD WE'VE NEVER MET

Most of us have been taught to believe in an all-powerful, omnipotent God
who is in charge of everything and everyone,
who coerces and controls us unilaterally,
who makes things happen according to God's will

so that every event we experience
fulfills a divinely predetermined future for our lives.

But this *all-powerful* God does not exist in the Bible.
This *all-controlling* God is not a rational construct.
This *omnipotent* God is not consistent
with our lived experience.

The ancient Hebrews never conceived of, spoke about,
or worshiped an omnipotent, all-controlling God.
It was only with the advent of Christianity
that we came to believe in this kind of God.

The early twentieth-century mathematician
and philosopher Alfred North Whitehead reminds us
where and when the Christian tradition departed
from ancient Jewish thinking about God:

> When the Western world accepted Christianity,
> Caesar conquered; and the received text of Western
> theology was edited by his lawyers. . . . The brief
> Galilean vision of humility flickered throughout the
> ages, uncertainly. . . . But the deeper idolatry, of
> the fashioning of God in the image of the Egyptian,
> Persian, and Roman imperial rulers, was retained.
> The Church gave unto God the attributes which
> belonged exclusively to Caesar.[6]

When Christianity became the official religion
of the Roman Empire,
it turned God into a unilaterally powerful Caesar
who sits on a throne,
throws his weight around,
dispenses judgments,
and imposes his might and will.

But the ancient Hebrews
had a much different view of God.

They had such a reverence for God's mysterious essence that they observed a commandment against depicting God in any artistic way: no graven images. Idols, statues, and religious effigies were human distortions of God that diminished God's true essence.

They understood the same to be true of human language. No single word could fully encapsulate the nature and essence of God.

But that didn't stop them from trying to describe God. They came up with many names for God, but two names appear most frequently in Hebrew Scripture.

The first and most common name for God is Yahweh, which early Christian interpreters translated as "the Lord." It's a name that many believe points to God's sovereignty and authority. This translation perpetuates the misguided impression that God sits at the top of a cosmic "org chart," limited by nothing, accountable to no one.

But Yahweh means simply, *I Am*, or *I Am What I Am*.

The ancient rabbis believed Yahweh was not a noun but a verb form that expresses past, present, and future tenses all at once. They said YHWH means something like *the one who was-is-will be*.

I Am is everywhere, in all things, in every moment, for all time.

But there's another name for God in Hebrew Scripture, and how we've translated this name for God has created a lot of problems for how we've come to understand how God works in the world.

The Hebrew word for this name of God is *Shaddai*. It appears at least 48 times in Hebrew Scripture and is most often translated as *Almighty*.

The full expression is, *El Shaddai*, which Christians have traditionally translated as *God Almighty*.

It's from this simple but highly debatable translation that a concept completely foreign to the Hebrew mindset came to be. For centuries, Christian theologians have referred to this concept as God's omnipotence, from the Latin, *omni*, meaning *all*, and *potens* meaning *powerful*.

This omnipotent, Almighty God
has the power to coerce,
control,
manage,
even micromanage
everything that is happening and will ever happen and even intervening to prevent things that might happen.

But divine omnipotence was never a Hebrew concept.

Shaddai is from the Hebrew root word, *Shad*, meaning *breast*. The Hebrews translated the name *El Shaddai* not as *God Almighty*, but as *The Breasted God*.[7]

Can you envision the divine as *The Breasted God* who desires to embrace and hold you like a mother or a father, to nourish and care for you
with a deep and abiding love?

It's this tender, evocative image of *The Breasted God* that captured the heart and imagination and teaching of Jesus, who never once spoke of God as almighty or omnipotent. When he taught his disciples to pray, he told them: "Pray like this: 'Our Father …'"[8]

Abba was the Aramaic word he used for father.
The God of Jesus was *Abba*,
Daddy,
Papa,
a tender parent
who desires intimacy,

persuades us in love,
exercises not unilateral, but relational power.

To suggest that God is not omnipotent is not to render God powerless. God's unbounded, sovereign power is one of persuasive, relational love, rather than a controlling, coercive, unilateral force.

LOVE ACTUALLY

The apostle Paul, an early Christian leader, once wrote that love is patient and kind, never self-seeking, never insisting on its own way, but always supportive, loyal, hopeful, and trusting.[9]

True love is never coercive. True love lures, coaxes, calls and persuades us to that which is beautiful and liberating.

Do you remember that fable of Aesop—the one in which the North Wind and the Sun are arguing about which of them is the strongest? To settle the argument, they decide to test their strength on a traveler coming down the road. Which of them could get the traveler to remove his cloak faster?

The North Wind blasts his cold wind down upon the traveler, but the harder he blows, the tighter the man holds onto the cloak. Then the Sun calmly says to the North Wind, "Step aside," and proceeds to send a little heat upon the traveler, who loosens his cloak as he becomes increasingly warmer. And when the Sun turns up the heat by shining with full power, the traveler eventually removes his cloak before continuing on his journey.

Aesop didn't say it, but I'm pretty sure this was when the Sun dropped the mic.

It's one of the oldest lessons in the book: persuasion is a more powerful force than coercion.

Think for a moment about your own relationships that you would characterize as truly loving—those with spouses, partners, parents, children, siblings. In these relationships, we know that genuine love does not mean control or coercion. Genuine love means the opposite of control. It means letting go, relinquishing control, granting freedom and agency to the other.

Parents learn this truth over time. There's a limit to a parent's power to control and coerce their children. Wielding unilateral power over them might work, at least imperfectly, for a while. But eventually, children grow up and parents soon learn that they cannot control them, that all they really have is the power to persuade their children—to woo, call, coax them toward the good, toward their greatest potential and best possibilities.

Parents voluntarily step back to allow their children to be who they are and to become what they could be—with all the risks and potential for failure and tragedy that freedom entails. In that moment, both parents and their children equally accept the vulnerabilities and possibilities for suffering, disappointment, fulfillment, and joy.

Like God in the creation story, all parents can do is speak into the chaos, the *tohu va-vohu* of their children's lives, uttering their hopes and dreams for them, luring them toward the good.

This is how God works in our lives and in the world—calling, beckoning, wooing us in persuasive love.

ARE YOU LISTENING?

A grief-stricken woman came to my office in tears one afternoon. Her 38-year-old son came home from work the night before, stepped out of his car, and collapsed on the garage floor from a fatal heart attack.

Her son's sudden death led her to question
whether God was good, whether God was even real.

When my son died, she said, God died.

She told me she couldn't come to church anymore.
But the more we talked, she came to the conclusion
that what she really needed most was her church family
and friends—only she wasn't sure she could
sit in church with all her doubts and anger and
unanswerable questions.

I proposed an alternative. Come to church,
but don't come inside—at least not right away.
You can stay in your car the whole time.
When the service starts, someone can open the doors
so you can hear what's going on inside.

It was a storefront church in a strip mall,
with parking right outside the doors.

Park in front of the open doors.
Roll down the car window.
Just listen.
If you want to cry or
shake your fist at God or
scream or curse or question,
just roll up the window.

Every Sunday morning, for the next several weeks,
I could see her sitting in her car
with the window rolled down.

Occasionally, I saw her roll it up.

But eventually, she came inside.

I never asked her what it was that drew her back in.

Maybe she heard what the *tohu va-vohu* heard
on the first day of creation, "Let there be."

Maybe she heard the voice of the Divine Woo, saying
Psst!
You can do this!
You could be this!

Life after the God we can no longer believe in
can be one of the most fertile seasons for
claiming a life in pursuit of the God we have never met—
a God who loves us too much to coerce or control us,
a God who lures,
beckons,
persuades,
and woos us toward the divine dream,
calling us to becoming,
to goodness,
to beauty.

Chapter 3

"hmmm"

the aim of god

There's an ancient story about the moment the Hebrew people reached the shores of the Sea of Reeds after escaping slavery in Egypt. In this memorable scene, Moses raises his hand over the waters and the sea suddenly splits apart, allowing the Hebrew fugitives to walk through it on dry land as Pharaoh's pursuing army draws near. It's an epic liberation story that has forever defined the Jewish consciousness.

But some of the ancient rabbis taught that it might never have happened were it not for one relatively obscure figure who dared to act. As one rabbinical, noncanonical teaching imagined it, when the Hebrews reached the shores of the sea, the waters did not miraculously part at Moses' commanding gesture.

Instead, the leaders of all the tribes of Israel were debating and arguing about what to do next.

Mass confusion ensued. While nobody could agree on what their next move should be, everyone seemed to agree they had to do something.

Behind them was Pharaoh's marauding army.
In front of them an ostensibly impassable sea.
Trapped, with nowhere to go, they grew terrified.
Death seemed imminent.

At the height of desperation, a certain chieftain
from the tribe of Judah took a leap of faith.
His name was Nahshon ben Amminadab.
He was the first to step into the sea and start walking.
Following Nahshon's lead, the Israelites stopped arguing
with one another, entered the waters, and were saved.

The whole story might sound miraculous and mythological
were it not for the rabbis who later taught that the sea
didn't automatically part when Nahshon stepped into it.
It wasn't until the waters reached Nahshon's nose,
they said, that the sea finally split.

In popular Yiddish, to be a "Nahshon" means
to be an initiator.

The story of Nahshon ben Amminadab suggests that
God's dream for creation is not achieved
apart from the daring choices and actions of humans.
Someone had to go first.

Someone *always* has to go first.

And yet it's not inevitable that someone or anyone *will*
always go first.

Nahshon ben Amminadab, like all the Hebrews at the
water's edge that day, had an abundance of options before
him in that moment of truth. He could have
spoken up or fallen silent,
turned inward or turned around,
checked out or

bowed out or
waited out the whole situation.

No one knew what he was going to do.

Not even God knew what Nahshon would do.

There's a common misconception in popular Christianity
that holds that God has a pre-determined plan for our lives
and that God has preordained our future, orchestrating
every event of our past to conform to that future,
already knowing the decisions we will make in
every moment but giving us multiple choices
in the present only to test our faith because
behind every trial, every problem, every seemingly
impassible sea is a divine implanted purpose.

Within this framework,
Psst!
becomes
Pfft!

You *could* do this
turns out to be
You *will* do this.

You *could* be this
is really
You *will* be this.

PURPOSES OR PUPPETS?

This concept of a preordained, divinely planned future is
based loosely on a handful of passages from the Bible
suggesting that

> *before God formed us in the womb God knew us and*
> *consecrated us*[1] *and*
> *even the hairs of our head are all numbered*[2] *and*

even before a word is on our tongue, God knows it
*   altogether*[3] *and*
in God's book were written all the days of our life, when
*   none of them as yet existed*[4] *and*
all things work together for good.[5]

As a pastor, I've seen how this irreconcilable mash-up of divine omnipotence (God's all-powerfulness) and divine omniscience (God's all-knowingness) make belief in God profoundly disillusioning by turning God into the author and orchestrator of

abuse,
assault,
trauma,
suicide,
accidents and tragedies,
mass shootings,
natural disasters,
war,
global warming,
depression and anxiety,
physical and mental illnesses,
chronic suffering and deadly diseases.

It can also make belief in God infuriatingly paralyzing by turning God's unknowable will into a guessing game. When we find ourselves at a major crossroads, facing a weighty, consequential decision, we might feel incapable of acting decisively without some assurance that *everything will work out according to God's plan.*

Or when we've endured a major setback or deep disappointment or terrible loss and we're trying to make sense of it, we might be left wondering if it all happened for a reason, or how it all could possibly be part of God's plan.

Christians often try to make sense of events or
experiences or outcomes by saying,

> "There's a divine purpose for everything" or
> "All things work together for good for those who
>   believe" or
> "God's ways are not our ways" or
> "Someday we'll understand what today seems
>   incomprehensible."

And because our lives can feel so random
and out of our control, maybe it's comforting
to believe in a God who has a personalized master plan
all worked out for us—a plan that someday
will make sense of all the wonderful and beautiful things,
and even the tragic and terrible things, that happen to us.

But for many, all this talk about God's so-called plan
can seem confusing, even troubling.
When they look at the world or their lives,
all they can see is randomness, chance, coincidence.
Or worse, they see how their future has unfolded
in ways that made God seem absent
or even merciless and cruel.

It's hard enough that bad things happen,
but even harder still to imagine that there could be
a preordained reason for it.

Your pregnancy ends in a sudden miscarriage or
your marriage ends in a bitter divorce or
your dream job ends with a crushing layoff or
your child is born with a chronic or terminal disease or
your best friend's life ends in tragedy or
a tsunami claims hundreds of thousands of lives.

Many people struggle to believe that such experiences
could ever be part of God's plan,
so they stop believing altogether.

Others find deep consolation in their belief that God has a purpose for causing or allowing these bad things to happen. They may not understand why, but they believe all events in their lives unfold according to a perfect, divinely conceived plan. They believe whatever happens—for better or worse—reflects the will and unsearchable plans of God.

DIVINE BRAINSTORMING

There's a popular passage in the Bible that seems to speak of God's so-called plan. It's found in the book of Jeremiah. It's often at the top of the *Scripture's Greatest Hits* chart for a lot of Christians because it drips with confidence and divine promise that God knows and holds our future.

The famous passage is a proclamation of hope, spoken through the prophet Jeremiah, to the Jews who were living in exile in Babylon. It must have come to them at just the right time. They seemed futureless as a people. They had lost the war, and in losing the war, they lost everything else—their homes, their temple, their community, their sacred traditions and practices. Many lost their faith in God.

It was a catastrophe on a national and deeply personal scale. Their future—once believed to be so secure in God's hands—was now uncertain and precarious as they waited out their captivity 500 miles from home in a god-forsaken land called Babylon.

They openly lamented:
How could this happen to us?
What will happen to us?
Will it ever get better?

Into this spirit and season of collective despair, Jeremiah speaks these now familiar, oft-quoted words:

For surely I know the plans I have for you, says the LORD, plans for your welfare and not for harm, to give you a future with hope.[6]

There's that complicated word: *plans.*

It sounds like God has everything under control.
The future is set in stone.
God has it all planned out and
worked out and
everything from here on out
will work out
according to the plan God has for us.

Many people find this comforting.

But there is one glaring problem with this traditional interpretation.

The word *plan* doesn't appear anywhere in the original Hebrew version of this passage.

What Christians over the centuries have translated as *plan* in the Hebrew is *machashabah*. It means thoughts,
ways,
intentions.

To the ancients living in Babylonian captivity, it sounded something like, *For I know the thoughts or intentions that I think toward you.*

It's like God is saying,
"Hmmm, I have something in mind for you, some hoped-for aim for your life."

Time, history, your life, and mine—it's all heading somewhere. It's all moving toward some purpose, some aim or intention that God has in mind for us.

The nineteenth-century abolitionist minister Theodore Parker once captured the nature and shape of this aim when he suggested that there is a "moral arc of the universe" which, though difficult to calculate or see, can be divined by conscience. Parker was confident that this moral arc of the universe "bends toward justice."[7]

Parker named what we all sense
but often struggle to name: that the universe
is heading somewhere good and purposeful.

History marches and
tumbles and sometimes
stumbles toward some
higher, ultimate good.

Parker called that higher, ultimate good freedom and justice and equality.

The prophet Jeremiah called it *shalom.*

What is *shalom*?

The Hebrew word *shalom* means *peace.* But *peace* is an inadequate translation. We think of peace as the absence of conflict. But *shalom* is far more than the absence of conflict because we can be conflict-free and still lack a sense of peace. We might still be unsettled. We might still feel as if something is missing in our lives.

Shalom means to make something whole.

Shalom is an experience of fullness, completeness, contentment.

Perhaps the closest word to *shalom* in the English language is something like *well-being.*
But even that's inadequate, because *well-being* doesn't come close to capturing the radical and counterintuitive nature of *shalom.*

In the Hebraic way of thinking, this fullness, completeness, contentment, well-being called *shalom* is the result of the joining together of opposites or ostensibly opposing forces.

There's a popular vision of this joining together of opposites in the Hebrew Bible. It's found in the teachings of the ancient prophets that speak of what the world will be like when the messiah comes—like this one from Isaiah:

> The wolf shall live with the lamb;
>   the leopard shall lie down with the kid;
> the calf and the lion will feed together,
>   and a little child shall lead them.
> The cow and the bear shall graze;
>   their young shall lie down together;
>   and the lion shall eat straw like the ox.
> The nursing child shall play over the hole of the asp,
>   and the weaned child shall put its hand
>   on the adder's den.
> They will not hurt or destroy
>   on all my holy mountain,
> for the earth will be full of the knowledge of the LORD
>   as the waters cover the sea.[8]

Things we'd consider complete opposites—all in one place, at peace in each other's presence?

We'd say, "There's no way *these* opposites can coexist."

> Wolves and lambs?
> Leopards and goats?
> Toddlers and snakes?
> Liberals and conservatives?
> Oath Keepers and pacifists?
> *Even Coke and Pepsi drinkers?*

We'd call it a pipe dream.

But the prophets said it *would* happen—wholeness, well-being, *shalom*—when the messiah comes.

This is where the universe is headed.
This is the aim or intention for all of creation.
This is the *thought* God has in mind for us.

The moral arc of the universe bends
toward this ultimate purpose.

But it does not bend on its own.

God gives to each of us the task of bending it.
Shalom begins with us. But before it begins with us,
it must happen *in* us.

God has this *thought* in mind for us: that the opposites
within *us* would be joined together.

COMING AND GOING

Have you ever noticed how, whenever Jews greet or
welcome someone *and* whenever Jews say farewell to
someone, they use the same word—*shalom*?

The same word, *shalom*, is spoken whether you are
coming or going. In two of the most opposite situations
in life, arriving and departing, Jews use the same
word—*shalom*.

Shalom links beautifully all our
comings and goings
in one place,
in one moment,
joining together all our
yesterdays and tomorrows
in this one day called
today,
uniting what has been and what has yet to be,
the events and experiences of our past and the promises
and possibilities of our future,

in this one moment we call
now.

Are you at peace—*shalom*—with yourself right now?

If you're lacking a sense of wholeness or well-being in your life, chances are you're trying to separate your past and your future in ways that are crippling your present. The two must be joined to experience genuine peace and well-being.

William Faulkner famously said, "The past is never dead. It's not even past."

But we pretend it is. And it leads to a lot of un-peace in our lives and in our world.

America's original sin of slavery is not dead. It's not even past. It still haunts us in the forms of systemic racism and white supremacy and Christian nationalism.

In contrast, Nelson Mandela launched South Africa's Truth and Reconciliation Commission in 1995 to help heal his country and bring about a reconciliation of its people by uncovering the truth about human rights violations that had occurred during the period of apartheid. It sought to gather evidence and uncover information—from both *victims* and *perpetrators*—rather than to prosecute individuals for past crimes. Mandela understood that the past is never past.

Our past determines our present and informs our future possibilities. We are products of our past. We are the sum total of our past choices and experiences, and the sum total of the world's past choices and experiences.

There's an old country music ballad that says,

> Yesterday is dead and gone
> And tomorrow's out of sight
> And it's sad to be alone
> Help me make it through the night.[9]

It's a sad song made only sadder because it's not true: yesterday isn't really dead and gone. Nor is tomorrow out of sight. While we are the sum total of our past, we are always more than the totality of our past. The future remains open to the choices we have yet to make.

In this very moment, you and I are the products of our past—every past action, decision, experience, and occasion. We humans make, on average, 35,000 decisions a day.

Some of those decisions are trivial:
Will I eat Cap'n Crunch or Lucky Charms for breakfast?
Will I wear stilettos or flip flops?
Will I swipe right or swipe left?

Some decisions are much weightier:
Will I ask her to marry me?
Will I go to this college or that one?
Will I become a doctor or a welder or a bomb-tester?

35,000 decisions a day.
2,000 decisions per hour.
One decision every two seconds.

At this moment in my life, I am the product of about 677 million choices that I've made since my birth. Some of those 677 million decisions were brilliant. Others were suspect. A lot were fairly inconsequential. There were also a lot of choices made for me by other people—some of whom had my best interests in mind and others who didn't. Some of their decisions were wonderful. Others were awful.

We are all a present compilation of our past choices: good choices and bad choices, wins and losses, breakthroughs and setbacks, successes and missteps.

Sometimes we seized the day.
Sometimes the day seized us.

And yet here we are.

Jeremiah was speaking to a people who had
made some terrible choices—
they had worshipped false gods,
neglected the sick and the poor,
took bribes,
got off track,
lost sight of the aim God had set before them.

Before they knew it, they found themselves in exile,
far from home, far from God's *shalom*.

But Jeremiah sends an oracle that says
your past isn't final.
God still has this thought in mind for you,
this purpose for your *shalom*.
It's not too late.
It's never too late.

THE FUTURE IS WIDE OPEN

The late preacher and civil rights activist John Claypool
once said, "One of the most important decisions you'll
ever make is what to do with the past. Will it be one thing,
or everything?"[10]

Our past is never dead. But our past does not have to be
everything or all-determining. And if true *shalom* can only
happen when we join opposites, we can only find true
wholeness when our imperfect past meets the new, future
possibilities God is offering us in the here and now.

Shalom is refusing to get mired too deeply in the past and
refusing to live too far into the future.

The nineteenth-century Danish existentialist philosopher
Søren Kierkegaard once noted that a great source of
our unhappiness in life is our reluctance to let go of our

less-than-ideal past and our unwillingness to hope for anything less than an ideal or perfect future for ourselves. Unhappy people, he suggested, are those who have their *ideal*—that is, the essence of their being—in some manner outside of themselves and thus remain absent from themselves in the present moment. To be truly happy and fully present to ourselves in the here and now, argued Kierkegaard, we must look not to the remembered or the anticipated *ideal* but to a past that was real and a future that can be grounded in the real.[11]

Shalom, wholeness, well-being happens when we join our imperfect, less-than-ideal past with the more hopeful and real possibilities of the future and choose to live most fully in the real and present moment, deciding today who we will be, how we will live, whether we will pursue the aim or intention God has set before us.

God gives us a choice in the matter of how our futures will unfold. The paint on the canvas of our lives is never quite dry. Not even God knows our future. God knows completely everything that has ever occurred in our past. God knows completely every possibility for us in our present. But God does not know our future. Our future does not exist until we create it.

And there are always three powers at work in the creation of our future.

The first is the power of our past, which reminds us that where we've been and what we've experienced make a profound difference in who we can become. We do not exist in a vacuum. We take the creative influences of the past into ourselves in every moment.

The second is the power of God in every present moment, who is constantly offering us new possibilities of becoming that are unlike any other possibilities we've ever seen before. God creates these new, emerging possibilities based on the aim or intention or, as Jeremiah calls it, the *thought* God has in mind for us. God woos us, lures us, beckons us toward this aim, offering a way of dealing with our past, maximizing our experience of *shalom* in the present, and creating greater potential for achieving our aim in the future.

And the third power is ourselves. We decide what we will do, how we will live, who we will become. We are responsible for joining the actual past received from the world and the possible future received from God.

BURNING BUSHES EVERYWHERE

There's an ancient story about the day Moses was tending Jethro's flocks in the wilderness and the angel of the Lord appeared to him in a flame of fire out of a bush. Moses looked, and the bush was blazing, yet it did not turn to ash. Moses was commanded to remove his sandals from his feet, *for the place on which you are standing is holy ground.*[12]

Some of the rabbis who taught on this story centuries ago believed that this bush that burned but was not consumed was not a bush at all, but Moses' very life. In the wilderness of Midian, Moses saw himself—his real, true self. He saw the person he used to be, and the fiery passion he once had. He saw the past he'd been running from, and the destiny he left behind in Egypt. He saw the self that once burned with compassion for his people.

In the bush, he saw that his fire had not gone out after all. This is the real miracle of the story. As Moses was drawn to the flames of fire, he was drawn back to his self, back to the heart of fire that once defined his destiny.

The ancient sages drew a linguistic connection between the *flame of fire* (the Hebrew for *flame* is *lavah*) and a *heart of fire* (the Hebrew for *heart* is *lev*).

A flame burned within Moses' heart
that had never gone out—
his deep, instinctive opposition to the slavery in Egypt,
his love for his people,
his calling to liberate them.
This was the message that emanated from the inextinguishable flames,
the awareness that arose in his burning heart of fire.

In the flames of the burning bush, Moses' past met the possibilities of his future.

There are burning bushes all around us.
Some are telling us that something isn't right
with the world.
They're calling us to stop turning away, to choose to do what is right, to keep our eyes open,
in every moment, to this creative, collaborative process of joining together the power of the past, which is the power of the world, the power of the future, which is the power of God, and the power of the present, which is our own power to integrate these influences into who we are becoming in every moment.

We are always free to take these three creative powers and to use them as we wish. We can choose to take the best possible next move or not.

The choice is always ours. Whether we take the best possible next step or a step that is less than ideal, these three powers will always be at play in the next moment. Each will look differently than they did in the previous moment, based on which step we took. But the process is ongoing, never ending, which makes the possibilities for the future ever hopeful.

MULTIPLE CHOICE

An improbable mentor once taught me that we are rarely presented with exclusively good choices and bad choices—as if, at any given moment in our lives, there's only one right and faithful possibility among an abundance of wrong and unfaithful ones from which to choose and act upon. Instead, we're most often given a multitude of possibilities from which to choose—some of which are better than others, but the vast majority of which are faithful possibilities.

Years ago, as I wrestled with so many doubts and questions, a man appeared outside my office. It was a late Friday afternoon. The church office was already closed, the doors were already locked. He stood politely at the glass door knocking, peering in long enough to see me peering out at him with curiosity and annoyance.

His suit was three sizes too big.
His dark, weathered face looked like an old treasure map, wrinkled and worn.
He had only about a half-dozen teeth, which gave him a slight whistle when he spoke.
He wore a purple cap gracefully on his head, like a crown.

He'd come from a local shelter. He was homeless.

What I expected would be just another request for money turned out to be the beginning of an unlikely friendship that lasted for years.

He said, "The Lord has instructed me to visit you."

I said, "Umm, OK."

"The Lord," he said, "has sent me to pray with you, pastor."

I wondered why the Lord hadn't informed me first, but I said, "OK."

We talked for more than an hour. He never asked me for money or food or bus tokens. He only asked, as he turned to leave, if he could lay his hand on my head and give me a blessing.

I said, "OK?"

And then he laid his ancient, calloused hand on my head, and he blessed me.

A month later, he returned.
We talked.
And then he laid his hand on my head and blessed me.

The next month,
and every month for the next three years,
he'd take a bus to my office,
we'd talk,
and then he'd bless me.

His name was Thomas. He'd once been a popular preacher in Detroit until, as he said, *he lost his way*. When he finally found his way again, he turned to preaching in the shelters and on the streets—and once a month, he'd preach to me in the suburbs.

On one of Thomas' monthly visits, as I was facing a major life decision upon which it seemed my whole future depended, I laid out all my options and asked my wise and generous street-preaching house-less friend for some pastoral advice.

I confessed to him my fear of making the wrong decision, and in his customary whistle-speak Thomas said there *are* no wrong decisions and
that he was living proof that
even what might seem like wrong turns
can always lead to the right place.

And I told Thomas that may be true, but still, if it's not too much to ask, I'd really like to avoid sleeping in a homeless

shelter, and maybe there's a way to get to the right place
by a more direct, less inconvenient, route.

And Thomas laughed and said,
"There's always more than one road to get you
where you want to go,
you just have to choose a way and
only after you've chosen *that* way will God open
another way,
and then you choose again,
and it just goes on and on,
so stop worrying, pastor, and
just choose and
just trust and
just keep your eyes open."

And then he put his ancient, calloused hand
on my head and
he blessed me.

I WANT TO BREAK FREE

The apostle Paul beautifully articulated this continuous
interplay of the power of our past, the power of God, and
the personal power we possess to choose what is best
for us. He acknowledged that to be human is to desire the
aim—the thought God has in mind for us. We may even
know, through intuition or the law, what the next best step
is for us. But we still struggle with our choices. We do not
always do the right thing because other forces are at work
within us and from outside of us: selfishness, envy, greed,
pride, indolence, to name a few.

Paul describes this daily inner conflict to choose what
is best for us as slavery. He confesses that the good he
wants to do he often does not do, and the not-so-good he
doesn't want to do he often ends up doing.[13]

And yet he never concedes the struggle.
God's power to offer new possibilities is limitless.
The aim, the good thought God has in mind for us,
continues to woo us forward.

In every moment, God works with the settled material of
our past and the raw possibilities for our future, wooing
us, persuading us, to pick up the brush and fashion beauty
in the present moment.

For years, my kids have watched the long-running TV
show *The Office*. For a dozen straight years, it seems like
it's on every time I walk in the room. I had never really
taken the time to consider why the show has been so
wildly popular, or why I always stop to watch.

Until recently, when it occurred to me that the show
is about our human lives—our humdrum, predictable,
sometimes boring, often mind-numbing lives that are
bewilderingly preoccupied with staplers, fax machines,
trivial staff development meetings, and predictable,
pedestrian *"that's what she said"* punch lines from idiot
bosses consumed with pranking unsuspecting coworkers
who are forced to wear suits and ties to work.
Every. Single. Day.

It's our greatest fear, isn't it? That our lives are slowly
being devoured by a whole week of Mondays. That the
future will never look any different than the past.

But here's this show—a documentary, actually—about
the drab and dreary office at the Dunder Mifflin Paper
Company, where people show up every day and, by some
miracle, find love, laughter, community, and even purpose
and meaning.

Pam Beesly sums it all up in the show's finale when she
says, "There's a lot of beauty in ordinary things. Isn't that
kind of the point?"[14]

The show is quirky. It's silly. It's often absurd. But it's also wonderfully honest and even strangely hopeful—almost as if this is what life could be, even should be, where it might all be headed: *shalom*, the joining together of opposites, the freedom to choose and experience true peace in the present moment.

There is a God in the Bible many of us have never met.

This God sees too much possibility within us
to confine our futures to a predetermined plan.

This God has a thought in mind for us,
a future of *shalom* for each of us,
and all of us together,
which we can experience in the now,
if only we dare to take the next best step.

Chapter 4

"sheesh"

the nature of god

Have you ever lost untold hours of your one precious life
mindlessly swiping through random videos on TikTok?

What starts out as an innocuous view of a swearing
African Grey parrot named Cairo
somehow leads to an assortment of videos
on Japanese origami dinosaurs,
quick-and-easy air fryer pasta recipes,
canines futilely attempting to fetch tennis balls
while wearing cone collars,
and a lip-syncing teenager from the Philippines
bopping her head to the bass-thumping rhythm
of a viral Millie B song.

All of which, as you well know, leads seamlessly
to an irresistible stream of heart-stopping videos
featuring fearless interlopers jumping unlawfully from
tall structures with parachutes strapped to their backs.

That, by the way, is called BASE jumping. And thanks to TikTok's bizarre algorithms, I recently discovered that BASE jumping is one of the fastest growing extreme sports in the world.

BASE is an acronym for buildings, antennas, spans, and earth, each referring to the four types of launching pads from which irrational people choose to jump.

For BASE jumpers, no tall, fixed object is off-limits: downtown skyscrapers, catenaries, bridges, cliffs, towers, church steeples—it's all fair game.

Most jumps are taken from a height of 400 feet or less, which means, after jumping, you have about two seconds of free-falling pleasure before you must pull the cord on your parachute.

Failing to pull the cord in a timely manner invariably turns BASE jumping into what members of the BASE-jumping community probably call THUD jumping.

Swiping through countless BASE-jumping videos, I stumbled across a handful of clips featuring people leaping from the most unexpected of all launching pads: the Christ the Redeemer statue in Rio de Janeiro—that massive stone effigy of Jesus gracefully extending his arms over the crowded, cluttered city below.

The iconic statue stands more than 100 feet tall, on a small mountain that raises it up another 200 feet.

Someone actually looked up at that statue one day and thought it would be a major adrenaline rush to jump from the arms of Jesus.

But because leaping from the arms of Jesus is illegal in Rio, jumpers must climb the massive statue in the early morning hours, under the cover of darkness. Upon arrival, they carefully climb out onto the outstretched arms of Christ, and then take a leap of faith—freefalling for 2.5

seconds before pulling the cord on their chute and gliding safely back to earth.

It's a compelling, evocative image.

Leaping from the arms of Jesus.

I've known many people who have leapt from the arms of Jesus. Not with parachutes strapped to their backs but with backpacks stuffed with so many doubts and questions that went unanswered, silenced, and condemned for so long that they finally abandoned their faith altogether.

They took a leap of doubt—
which is actually a leap of faith away from faith—
away from the God they had always been told about but could no longer reconcile with their real, lived experience, away from the God who had ossified into something like a stone-cold effigy that was no longer life-giving or lifesaving:
a God who became as cold and
impassible and
immutable and
unresponsive
as granite.

Have you ever wondered how, if God never actually changes, it could ever be said that God is personal, loving, caring, or involved in our lives?

It's a question almost as old as time itself. Does God, like humans—like all creation—ever experience feelings, or a change of heart or mind, or a change of plans, or even a change in nature?

Or is God what Aristotle once called the
Unmoved Mover—
the initial, primary cause
that once set the universe in motion but ever since

has sat idly by,
uninvolved in and
unmoved by
the events of the world or
the circumstances of our lives?

Or is God what Isaac Newton and René Descartes
once called the Divine Watchmaker—
the cosmic intelligence that
designed and ordered the universe with
mechanical perfection,
according to certain physical and natural laws,
but who stands outside of space and time?

In an ever-changing world,
the notion of an unchanging God can be of great comfort.
The great world spins and weaves and wobbles,
but God forever remains the same.

A handful of passages from the Bible support this view:

"I, the LORD, do not change," says Malachi.[1]

"Every generous act of giving … is from above, coming down from the Father of lights, with whom there is no variation or shadow due to change," says James.[2]

"Jesus Christ is the same yesterday and today and forever," says Hebrews.[3]

This notion of an unchanging God is called the doctrine of immutability. It's based on the belief that, if God were to change, God would be imperfect, unreliable, untrustworthy.

The changeless perfection of God is what seemingly makes God worthy of our worship and reverence.

It's captured in a popular Christian hymn that sings of God's enduring steadfastness:

Great is Thy faithfulness, O God my Father,
There is no shadow of turning with Thee.
Thou changest not, Thy compassions, they fail not.
As Thou hast been, Thou forever wilt be.[4]

If you can get beyond all the
Thous, Thys, and Thees,
you get the point: God's as solid as a rock.

That can be a source of comfort and assurance for those
who want a reliable God who is in control of everything.

But it's an obstacle for those who long
for a relational God who
cares deeply about our lives,
responds to our needs,
feels what we feel, and
is influenced by what we experience.

TURN AND FACE THE STRANGE

Have you ever been in any meaningful relationship with
anyone, for any length of time, who did not, or could not,
or would not change? How did it work out for you?

I met my wife, Lori, when we were both 16 years old.
If, at that time, Lori had any suspicion
that I'd still be bleaching my hair and playing *Pong*
on my Atari game console and still trying to get through
high school physics thirty-plus years later,
our first date would have been our last.

To be alive, to relate to anything alive in this world
with anything like love requires genuine change.

The effect that genuine love has in any relationship
is mutual.
Love changes the lover and the one who is loved.

If you've only ever known of a distant, unmoved, uncaring God, there's a God in the Bible I want you to meet—a God who, out of deep love, is constantly changing.

There are more than 40 passages in Hebrew Scripture that speak of a God who changes.

> And the Lord changed his mind about the disaster that he planned to bring on his people, says Exodus.[5]

> And the Lord was sorry that he had made humans on the earth, and it grieved him to his heart, says Genesis.[6]

> For their sake he remembered his covenant and showed compassion, says the Psalmist.[7]

> (I)f that nation, concerning which I have spoken, turns from its evil, I will change my mind about the disaster that I intended to bring on it, says Jeremiah.[8]

> The Lord relented, says Amos.[9]

Throughout Hebrew Scripture, we meet a God who
repents
regrets
relents
responds
receives
returns
renews
rejoices and
remembers.

And each of those re- words implies:
that God is involved in, and not standing outside of,
space and time; and
that God is in some way affected by, or influenced by,
creation because God stands within space and time.

There's an ancient story about a man named Abraham
who bargains with God. God intends to destroy Sodom,
a city that has become so corrupt that it seems
irredeemable even to God.

But Abraham is worried that there might be some
good, innocent people in Sodom who would perish
undeservedly, so he pleads with God.

Abraham asks God if there were fifty righteous people in
Sodom, would he spare the city?

God thinks it over and tells Abraham
that if he can find fifty righteous people,
God will spare Sodom for their sakes.

Abraham ups the ante. What about forty-five?
Would you spare the city for forty-five?

God thinks it over and agrees to spare the city
for forty-five.

But Abraham will not stop bargaining with God. What
about forty? Thirty? Twenty? Would you go as low as ten?

Abraham eventually wears God down,
until God finally relents. I'm pretty sure this was
the first time anyone in the world ever used the word,
Sheesh, and it was God who said it.

Sheesh.

The last line of the story says, *And the LORD went his way.*[10]

ESSENCE AND EXPERIENCE

The God we meet in the Hebrew Bible is not an
Unmoved Mover or *Divine Watchmaker*.
This God doesn't set everything in motion
and then sit back,

outside of space,
beyond time,
with arms folded,
casually, objectively, indifferently observing the world,
unaffected by it all.

This is a God who listens and discerns and experiences
our needs and circumstances in real time, with us, and
then responds according to God's divine nature.

This is a God who is all at once both
unchanging
and
changing.

To understand this paradox, it's necessary to distinguish
between God's essence and God's experience.[11]

God has both—just like you and me.

Consider your own life.
You are a human being.
You have been a human being all your life.
You have never been anything other than a human being.
For as long as you are alive,
you will always be a human being.

And we have a lot riding on the fact that you will never be
anything other than a human being, by the way.

But your experience as a human being has been
constantly changing over the course of your life,
moment by moment, from day to day, from year to year.
You are not the same human today that you were as a
newborn in that cute little onesie, or as a freshman in
high school when you had that pink mohawk, or even as
you were this morning when you rolled out of bed and
your feet touched the floor.

That human is history.

So is the human you were just a moment ago when you were reminiscing about that pink mohawk.

Your human essence *never* changes.
But your human experience is *always* changing.

This is true at the most basic, biological level of human existence. The human body is constantly undergoing change. It never stops dying and renewing itself.

At this very moment, there are about thirty-five to forty trillion cells occupying your body, but those cells are not all the same cells you had yesterday. Over time, some cells get old and tired; others get damaged; some even go on strike or mutate or self-destruct for reasons we can't explain.

Before they die, cells must replicate themselves. And it turns out they are highly efficient at creating their own replacements—about 330 billion—every day.

Some cells work on a much tighter timeline than others.

White blood cells live for about three days.
Red blood cells can last about four months.
Skin cells are good for about two weeks.
Bone cells regenerate every ten years.
Brain cells, sadly, do not regenerate at all.
Nor does your teeth enamel or the lenses of your eyes.
Fat cells, however, stick around for twelve to fifty years, which confirms the scientific accuracy of the phrase *stubborn belly fat*.

But even after all this cellular replacement, you're never really a whole new you. You're still the same human you've always been.

The same is true at the most complex, conscious level of human existence. Our minds are always changing. We are constantly taking in new information, novel experiences, emergent ideas, and *aha* moments that influence how we come to think about and interact with our world.

As we grow older, we discover indispensable, life-altering details about ourselves, about others, and about the world that make it possible for us to be more fully human, to make more informed choices, to be better people.

What are some of these helpful details that we learn over time?

Monsters do not actually live under our bed.
Muslims, like Jews and Christians, belong to one of the world's three Abrahamic religions.
If you close your eyes in a dark room, then open them, the color you see is called *eigengrau*.
People with the most friends outlive those with the fewest by 22 percent.
There are more life forms on the surface of your body than people on the surface of Earth.
People with culturally and politically diverse friends are, on average, happier and healthier.
Eating too much blue cheese can give you bad dreams.
Around 80 to 90 percent of people with depression respond positively to therapy.
"I.e." and "e.g." are not the same thing.
The level of carbon dioxide (CO_2) in Earth's atmosphere is now at its highest in two million years.
Showing tropical flower dieffenbachia uncensored footage of explicit pollination acts makes them bloom.
About 12.8 million Africans were abducted and shipped across the Atlantic over a span of 400 years.
The smell after it rains is called *petrichor*.

Some of this you probably already knew.
Some of this will not change your mind about anything.
Some of it might.
But you'll never look at blue cheese the same way again.
And probably not dieffenbachia, either.

Having this information will not change who you are because your human *essence* is constant.
But it may be useful to your human experience because your human *experience* is flexible, malleable, responsive, adaptable, always in flux as you interact with and learn about the physical world.

So it is with God.

God's essence is unchanging.
God's experience is ever-changing
because God takes in every new experience of the world and responds creatively in love.

UNCHANGING AND
EVER-CHANGING

The ancient Hebrews always understood this dual nature about God. While they steadfastly believed there was only one God, they had multiple names for God that sought to capture what they perceived to be the infinite, unchanging nature of God on the one hand, and the finite, ever-changing experience of God on the other.

The two Hebrew names for God that spoke of this complementary aspect of God were *Elohim* and *Adonai*. One God with two names. Both names are found throughout Hebrew Scripture, but how they appear in the ancient creation story—the first two chapters of Genesis—is telling.

The first name, *Elohim*, is found in the first chapter of Genesis, but not the second. The second name, *Adonai*, is found in the second chapter of Genesis, but not the first. What is the character of *Elohim* and *Adonai*?

Elohim is the ground of creation,

the everlasting, primordial, transcendent poet
of the world,[12]
the divine presence that precedes creation and envisions
and orders its possibilities,
whose spirit sweeps like a bird over the soupy, swirling
mess of preexistent chaos
and disorder—the *tohu va-vohu*—and, seeing some
hidden potential and possibility for life, beauty, order,
says "Let there be ..."

Elohim is the one who sees everything that could be
and whispers, "Psst,"
calling, wooing, all things to light and life.

Elohim is the one who sees everything that responds
to the divine calling,
everything that chooses to come to light and life,
and calls it all *very good*.

This is the essential, infinite, changeless nature of God.

But the second chapter of Genesis introduces another,
distinct name for God, *Adonai*, that speaks of God's finite,
ever-changing, relational, and experiential nature.

In the creation story of Genesis 2, *Adonai* is introduced
before there were plants of the field,
before the vegetation sprung up,
before the rain had ever fallen upon the earth,
before there was anyone to till the ground.

That's when *Adonai* "formed man from the dust of the
ground and breathed into his nostrils the breath of life,
and the man became a living being."[13]

Adonai is the consequent, persuasive divine power that
beckons reality to achieve its potential,
to pursue its highest ideal or aim,
to claim its agency and responsibility,
to collaborate with *Elohim*.

Elohim is the ground of the universe
that is self-given from God.
Adonai is the energy, the very breath, that infuses
and animates and transforms it.

Elohim works with the raw potential of the universe.
Adonai works in the transformation of that raw potential
toward God's highest intention.

Elohim is defined by divine sovereignty.
Adonai is defined by the divine-creation partnership.

Elohim is the God of all that is.
Adonai is the God of all that could be.

Both *Elohim* and *Adonai* are indispensable to the process
of sustaining creation and calling it to flourish. When
Elohim and *Adonai* are joined together in the ancient
creation poem, we are introduced to a God whose essence
is unchanging, yet whose experience with creation is
ever-changing.

Adonai Elohim.

Usually translated into English as *the LORD God,*[14] these
two names are commonly found side by side in Jewish
prayer books today as a reminder of this divine-human
partnership.

The world was created incomplete,
full of given potentialities that require creaturely
actualization.
God, *Elohim*, exists and calls and woos prior to creation,
and for creation.
God, *Adonai*, enters into relationship with us through
creation as we respond to God's call.

In this way, *Elohim* and *Adonai* are not distinct natures of
God, but interrelated and a part of the same process of
becoming as we are.

We experience *Adonai Elohim.*
Adonai Elohim experiences us.

Adonai Elohim calls.
We respond.
Adonai Elohim receives our response and calls again,
based on how we just responded.
We respond to the call, based on the new possibilities
Adonai Elohim presents to us.

God, *Adonai Elohim,* is changeless and ever-changing.

Sheesh.

NEVER-CEASING, EVER-NEW

Lamentations calls this dual nature of God *steadfast love.*

> The steadfast love of the LORD never ceases;
> his mercies never come to an end;
> they are new every morning;
> great is your faithfulness.[15]

Steadfast love is God's essence.
It never changes.
It's dependable, reliable, constant.

Steadfast love is also God's experience.
It's new every morning.
It's not yesterday's love.
It's different today.

Why?

Because if God's creative, persuasive love is to have its
fullest effect, achieving the highest good for us, that love
must always change, adapt, take in new information,
discern what effect it has had so far, and consider what
new possibilities might be best for us in this new moment.

This is God's experience—the aspect of God
that changes according to the day, the hour,
the moment of our own experience.

How does this *Adonai Elohim,*
unchanging-ever-changing,
steadfast love of God
work together?

The best we can do, perhaps, is compare God's steadfast
love to the kind of human love that characterizes our most
intimate, loving relationships—like that between a parent
and child.

Both of my sons grew up playing baseball. I also grew up
playing baseball and played competitive baseball into my
early forties.

There was a time when I knew a lot more about the
intricacies of the game than my sons did. I had some
knowledge and skills, and they had a genuine curiosity and
desire to learn. Because I have always loved them and
wanted the best for them, I taught them how to play.

When they were young, I bought a bat, a tee, a bucket
of balls, and a hitting screen. Nearly every day, often for
hours, I'd lob balls or throw them soft toss. I went easy on
them. Eventually, they learned how to hit.

As they grew older, my repertoire had to expand. They
needed more of a challenge. Soft toss and batting tees
would only get them so far. We had to get more creative.

We moved on to live pitching in a batting cage.
I threw them fastballs, curveballs, changeups.
I even threw some brushback pitches to keep them
honest. You get the point.

I did this because I love them and have always wanted
the best for them.

Did my love change? On the one hand, it didn't change at all. I always wanted the very best for them, and I always acted in ways that would help improve their skills and maximize their love for the game. This love was steadfast.

But on the other hand, my love really did change. When they were five years old, the most loving thing would not have been to throw four-seam fastballs or knuckle-curveballs to them. But when they were fifteen, I believed it was the most loving thing I could do for them.

That I love my sons is absolutely unchanging.
How I have loved them over the years, and love them still, is always changing.[16]

Our human analogies fall short whenever we speak of God's love. But it's something like that.

God's *steadfast love* never ceases.
God's *steadfast love* is new every morning.

Adonai Elohim is nothing like the God so many of us have struggled to comprehend—the so-called Unmoved Mover whom, we've been told, loves us only from an insurmountable distance.

Consider the story of Jesus' close friend Lazarus.[17] Lazarus is sick. His friend, Jesus, has a pretty good track record on making people well. But Jesus is out of town. He doesn't get there in time. Lazarus is dead on arrival.

Jesus loves Lazarus. When he's told that Lazarus is dead, Jesus feels the loss deeply. Jesus is *greatly disturbed in spirit and deeply moved.*

Jesus weeps.

An *Adonai Elohim* love that feels what we feel.

But after Jesus asks Lazarus' sisters to roll away the stone from Lazarus' tomb, he utters three of the most evocative words in all the Bible—

"Lazarus, come out!"[18]

And Lazarus comes out. On his own two feet.

It's a story about an *Adonai Elohim* kind of love that feels, internalizes, calls forward, woos, and waits for us to choose our next best step.

It's a story about the divine-human partnership that always requires a response for the *Adonai Elohim* love to have its fullest effect.

Sheesh.

There's a God in the Bible many of us have never met—
an *Elohim* whose steadfast love never changes or ceases,
an *Adonai* whose mercies are new every morning,
an *Adonai Elohim* who works and waits
for what is best for us.

Chapter 5

"hum"

the presence of god

I recently walked the celebrated Camino de Santiago, a major pilgrimage trail that leads to the shrine of the apostle James in the Cathedral of Santiago de Compostela in northwestern Spain. There, tradition holds, the relics of the apostle are buried.

I did not actually confirm this.

Pilgrims from all over the world have been walking the Way of St. James since at least the tenth century. Many follow the Camino's various routes as a form of spiritual practice or retreat for their spiritual growth, although most of the pilgrims I spoke with on the trail were walking the Camino for a variety of other, seemingly less spiritual, reasons.

Some were on sabbatical or between jobs.
Some were re-examining their priorities and commitments.

Some were grieving a divorce, or the loss of love,
or the loss of a loved one.
Some were facing a major life transition,
or a personal setback, or a life-changing illness.
Some were trying to get in shape or lose weight or,
as one pilgrim explained,
"I really just want to look good naked."

While most of them wouldn't quite say it this way, I think
they were all in some way, like me, walking the Camino
in search of answers or meaning or an epiphany or an
experience that might have at least hinted at what is often
meant when we talk about God.

Have you ever searched for God?

If you made a list of all our imaginative answers to
the question of where God can be found, you'd quickly
discover that our beliefs are all over the map—or, more
precisely, that God is all over the map.

God, we are told, is
up there,
down here,
out there,
in here,
over there,
everywhere,
elsewhere,
nowhere.

So we search for God by turning our gaze inward and
exploring the spiritual landscape of our lives through a
variety of spiritual practices like
prayer,
meditation and breathing exercises,
journaling,
yoga and tai chi,
spiritual direction,

fasting, or
contemplative reading.

Or we search for God by turning our gaze outward
and exploring those places where others have claimed
to have found God—
the ancient sites of the Holy Land,
the medieval cathedrals of Europe,
the Buddhist temples of Kathmandu,
the pilgrimage trails of Spain and Italy,
the silent monasteries of Greece,
the deserts of New Mexico or
the casinos of Las Vegas.

Some people claim to have found God in the strangest
places.

Like church.

But finding God in church, it seems, is becoming
increasingly rare.

For a growing number of people, their search for God
has led them *as far away from the church* as they can get.
Maybe that's because the God they met when they went
to church was nothing like the loving, luminous, numinous,
life-giving God they had hoped to find. In their search for
God, maybe they found religion instead of a relationship.

A lot of people do not know the difference between
religion and relationship.

There's an old joke that says
religion is a guy in church thinking about fishing and
relationship is a guy out fishing thinking about God.

Churches are often filled with people
thinking about fishing.
But the world is full of people out fishing
thinking about God.

Which reminds me of something I read about the actor Jane Fonda.

Fonda has blogged about her conversion to Christianity late in life. She said she had been an atheist all her life, but then she found herself in her 60s, at the end of her marriage with Ted Turner in 2001, and she realized how, all her life, she was always trying to be perfect so she could be loved.

She never felt whole. She described her experience as always feeling "dis-embodied."

But then something happened. She started to feel herself becoming whole. She found God.

She didn't describe her spiritual journey in conventional churchy language. But I think her beautiful and compelling story about how she came to the faith resonates with a lot of people today. She writes,

> My faith is a work in progress (as am I). But I will plant my flag on the belief that God lives within each of us as Spirit. . . . I believe that Christ was the personal incarnation of the divine wisdom in everything, including every form of spiritual expression.[1]

Responding to criticism over her decision not to follow "established religion" and her assertion that "God is beyond gender," Fonda says,

> Some will say that because of all this I am not a true Christian. So be it. I feel like a Christian, I believe in the teachings of Jesus and try to practice them in my life. I have found Christians all over this country who feel as I do. They may not have been 'saved' yet they hum with divine spirit.[2]

Have you ever hummed with divine spirit?

Have you ever had an experience in which you found yourself deeply aware of something beautiful or powerful? Something beyond what you can know and observe and describe rationally?

Have you ever sensed that there might be a presence *humming* behind the veil of reality, something unmistakably real but not altogether reasonable or explainable?

The late Frederick Buechner wrote about visiting Sea World in Orlando. Buechner, his wife, and their twenty-year-old daughter were watching a killer whale show where five or six whales were performing. This was years before most of us began questioning whether capturing marine mammals for theatrical purposes was ethical and humane.

But Buechner said the delight of the crowd appeared matched only by what seemed to be the delight of the whales. Something extraordinary happened. He said, "It was as if the whole of creation—men, women, beasts, sun, water, earth, sky and maybe even God himself—were caught up in a dance of unimaginable beauty,"[3] a dance of unmitigated light and shared joy.

Buechner realized, to his surprise, that his eyes had filled with tears, and after the show was over, he mentioned this experience to his wife and daughter, who said the same thing had happened to them.

> Caught up in a dance of unimaginable beauty.
> A dance of unmitigated light and joy.

I've heard of similar experiences from so many people— the sense that something is going on here that I can't explain, something moving, real, visceral.

For a growing number of spiritual but not religious people, there's an openness to the possibility that this *humming*, this *dance of unimaginable beauty*, might be God, or have something to do with God. They don't know how to quantify it, describe it, prove, or verify it.

It doesn't correspond to the modern standards of human reason and science.

It doesn't conform to the well-established doctrines of the Church.

But that doesn't mean it isn't real.

Is God up there, down here, out there, in here, everywhere, or elsewhere? If you said yes, you might be right—if being right is your objective.

But in the end, what really matters is:
Have you ever felt that hum?
Have you ever experienced that dance
of unimaginable beauty?
Are you experiencing God?

If we feel the hum, then do we need to be right or certain about anything?
If we don't feel the hum, is there any amount of being right or certain that can ever satisfy the deep longing we all have for experiencing God?

BREATHE A LITTLE LOVE

The ancient Hebrews had a word for that hum.
They called it *ruach*. You can translate it as *breath* or *spirit*.
For the Hebrews, *ruach* was both. God's breath was God's spirit.

Try this: hold your breath and say the word *ruach* at the same time. Don't worry, no one is looking. Just try it.

You couldn't do it, could you?

Uttering the word *ruach* requires you to engage your breath and lungs.

The first mention of *ruach* in the Bible is found in the very first chapter of Genesis:

> (T)he earth was complete chaos, and darkness covered the face of the deep, while a wind from God swept over the face of the waters.[4]

The word here for wind is *ruach*. God-breath. God-spirit. Divine exhalation sweeping over the primordial, soupy chaos, suffusing the *tohu va-vohu* with life, infusing the *tohu va-vohu* with God's essence.

The Genesis account of creation says everything that is has come to be because of an explosive, expansive, creative energy—*ruach*—humming and pulsing through all living things.

The Hebrews knew this almost intuitively, which is why, when we read the Bible, we never once find them sitting around, wondering, "*Is* there a God?"

There were times when they perceived that God was distant, or hiding, or slow to respond. But as long as they were breathing, they knew there was a God, and they knew where to find God.

What they *did* talk about was how all life, all living things—people, whales, sparrows, stars, fruit flies, dandelions—all life shared this singular, sustaining life force, which they called God.

The Hebrews had a name for this God: *YHWH*.

These four consonants, *Yod, Heh, Vav, Heh*, represented not only God's name, but God's essence.

Just like the word *ruach*, you can't say these four consonants while holding your breath.

If you've ever struggled with the popular image of God as a white-bearded old man sitting on a throne, high above creation, occasionally reaching down and tinkering with it, then consider this Hebrew belief that the God of the Bible is a God who is as close to you as your breath.

Ruach. Breath. Spirit.

The word *ruach* appears 378 times in the Hebrew Bible.

Its Greek counterpart, *pneuma*, appears 403 times in the New Testament.

Are you following this?

We have something like 781 references in the Bible to a God who is spirit or breath—an evocative, life-giving image of God.

At some point in history, it seems, some guys from the marketing department got together to decide how to brand this God character. They put a handful of really good ideas on the table: Spirit,
Shepherd,
Potter,
Law Giver,
Creator,
Abba,
Alpha and Omega,
to name a few.

But then a team from corporate marched in and declared that, based on current consumer trends, we really need to go with the *white-bearded Colonel Sanders elderly man wrapped in a swirling cloak* concept.

That settled it.

But *ruach*, *pneuma*, breath, spirit isn't just up there. It's everywhere.

Psalm 139 says,

Where can I go from your spirit?
  Or where can I flee from your presence?
If I ascend to heaven, you are there;
  if I make my bed in Sheol, you are there.
If I take the wings of the morning
  and settle at the farthest limits of the sea,
even there your hand shall lead me,
  and your right hand shall hold me fast.[5]

Up. Down. Here. There. Everywhere. Elsewhere. Anywhere.

It turns out that you don't have to go anywhere *in search of God*.

God's *ruach*, spirit, presence
will find you,
is with you,
is in you,
is already there before you even get there.

A man named Job endured unimaginable loss and suffering. Everything that meant anything to him was taken from him. He was up, down, here, there.

He questioned God's compassion, God's reasons, God's justice.

But, curiously, he never doubted God. He knew God had been and always would be with him.

God, he said, is the "spirit ... in my nostrils."[6]

EVERY BREATH YOU TAKE

Jesus once spoke of how God's *ruach* or *pneuma* works. His friend Nicodemus was searching for God, hoping even to capture God or pin God down. Jesus said it doesn't work that way.

"The wind [*pneuma*] blows where it chooses, and you hear the sound of it, but you do not know where it comes from or where it goes. So it is with everyone who is born of the Spirit."[7]

The apostle Paul once met some Greeks in Athens who were praying to a variety of gods. They were even praying to an altar with the inscription *to an unknown god*, because why not hedge our bets?

Paul told them the God they were searching for can't be fashioned into a tawdry figurine. The only God worthy of our prayers is the God who *"gives to all mortals life and breath."*[8]

When we understand—like the Hebrews, like Jesus, like the early Christians—that God is breath/spirit, we stumble across two very life-changing, world-impacting discoveries.

First, we discover that God is in us.

God exhales, and creation comes to life. God's spirit—God's very essence—enters us and all living things. Not the whole of God's essence—that would imply that you, your pet hedgehog, and your Japanese bonsai tree are all somehow God. This is called *pantheism*.

To say that God is *in* all things is not to say that all things are God. It's to affirm that God's *ruach/pneuma* is an intimate, inseparable part of us. It's in us, around us, moving through us. Every breath we take, every breath we're about to take, in every time and place, is God-breath, *ruach*, spirit, God's essence.

Science proves this out.

There's a scientific theory called Caesar's Last Breath, a classic teaching tool for high school and college students.

It's proven by a complicated mathematical formula. What it demonstrates is mind-blowing.

The theory of Caesar's Last Breath takes us back about 2,070 years, to that fateful day when Julius Caesar, the great conqueror, was stabbed in the Senate by his good friend Brutus.

And you thought the senate is harsh today. Brutus's politics were next level.

Mortally wounded, Caesar slumped over, took his last breath, and died.

Caesar's dying breath has become a classic teaching tool for chemistry professors.

What the theory of Caesar's Last Breath suggests is this: when Caesar exhaled his last breath in 44 BCE, he released an enormous number of breath molecules, mostly nitrogen and carbon dioxide.

How many molecules? To be exact, 10^{23}. It looks like this many molecules:

100,000,000,000,000,000,000,000

Scientists speculate about what would happen to all those molecules: some would be absorbed by plants, some by animals, some by water, and a large portion would float free and spread themselves all around the globe, in a pattern so predictable that, if you take a deep breath right now, at least one of the molecules entering your lungs literally came from Caesar's last breath.

And not only Caesar's breath, but every breath that has ever been taken by every living creature that has ever lived.

Earth's atmosphere contains all the air that ever was, every breath ever taken. Not a single atom or molecule

will ever slip through the atmosphere—unless, of course,
we happen to burn a hole through it. *Ahem.*

That means every creature, from the moment of creation
to this very moment today, shares the same breath.

We breathe in
the fetid breath of the brontosaurus
and the pungent effluvium of every blue whale,
the breath of Jesus of Nazareth and Mary Magdalene
and Judas Iscariot and Pontius Pilate,
the breath of Augustine and Aquinas and Anselm
and Hildegard of Bingen,
the breath of Joan of Arc and Attila the Hun
and Genghis Khan,
the breath of Shakespeare, Michelangelo,
Beethoven, and Rosa Parks,
the breath of Muhammad and Mother Teresa
and Ted Kaczynski and Pope Francis.

We breathe in
the breath of our best friend and our worst enemy,
the breath of our parents and grandparents,
the breath of our children and grandchildren.

And we breathe in the breath/*ruach*/*pneuma* of God that
swept across that soupy chaos on the first day of creation.

The ancient Hebrews, Jesus, and the early Christians all
knew this. They didn't need a scientific theory to prove it.

Others, from non-Christian traditions,
have also known this.

The ancient Greek philosopher Plotinus said, "All events
are coordinated. All things depend on each other.
Everything breathes together."[9]

"I am creating a mortal out of potter's clay of black mud
altered," says the Qur'an. "So, when I have made him and
have breathed into him of My spirit . . ."[10]

Mahatma Ghandi sensed this hum of the divine spirit. He felt an indefinable, mysterious power pervading everything he experienced. He said, "I feel it, though I do not see it. It is this unseen power that makes itself felt and yet defies all proof.... It transcends the senses."[11]

Jesus was right. The spirit didn't belong to the Jews or to any religious system. "The [spirit] blows where it chooses, and you hear the sound of it, but you do not know where it comes from or where it goes."

It's like when you breathe on the palm of your hand.
You can feel it.
You can't *see* your breath,
but you can feel it as it flows over your skin.
It's both tangible and intangible.
You can sense it and feel it,
but you can't hold it or contain it or even direct it.

So it is with God.

The divine spirit breathes in us,
for us,
with us.

If the essence of God is in all living things, shouldn't that influence how we perceive ourselves, knowing that we are not God, but that God is in us?

If the spirit of God is in and breathing with all living things, shouldn't that influence how we relate to the world, knowing that the earth is not God, but that God's spirit is in the soil, the oceans and rivers, the blue-tailed skink, the grey wolf, the western pronghorn, the cutthroat trout?

As Nikos Kazantzakis once wrote, "Blowing through heaven and earth, and in our hearts and the heart of every living thing, is a gigantic breath—a great Cry— which we call God."[12]

Do you see it? Do you feel it? The hum, reverence, *ruach*, *pneuma*?

BREATHE OUT SO I CAN BREATHE YOU IN

When we understand that God is in all living things, we make one other important discovery—that all living things are in God. We are a part of God's experience. All things are in God. Some theologians call this *panentheism*.

This can be a difficult concept for some people to comprehend.

When God exhales, God's *ruach*/*pneuma*/spirit enters all living things.
But a full breath is both exhalation *and* inhalation.

When God breathes in, our spirit, or essence,
is taken into God.

God experiences us.
God is influenced by our experiences.
God is in all things.
All things are in God.

The thirteenth-century Persian poet Rumi once said, "You are not a drop in the ocean, you are the ocean in a drop."

God is in us. We are in God.

One of the last prayers of Jesus was that his followers might live as those who are in God's experience.
"As you, Father, are in me and I am in you,
may they also be in us."[13]

How does this work with God?

All we have are human analogies to help us. But try this:

Make a list of all the significant moments or events
that have ever influenced your life.
The birth of a child,
the death of a parent,
the time you got fired,
cashing your first paycheck,
taking a road trip with friends,
falling in love,
running a marathon,
and that one awkward situation with the clogged toilet
at your girlfriend's house back when you were in high
school.

If it makes your list of memorable events, it's because you
experienced it. In some way, you are still experiencing it.

Consider all the people who have ever influenced you
in some positive or negative way—
spouses and siblings,
parents and grandparents,
children and grandchildren,
friends and mentors,
allies and adversaries,
difficult people and hurtful people, and
the stranger who stopped to help you that one day
on the side of the highway.

If they made your list of influential people, it's because you
have experienced them. You are still experiencing them.
They are in your ongoing experience.

I can remember sitting in the backseat of my parents' 1978
Ford Thunderbird on a summer afternoon in Southern
California, listening to Neil Diamond on the 8-track with
the window rolled down as my whole family sang "Sweet
Caroline" at the top of our lungs. I was ten years old. I
remember in that moment feeling safe and accepted and
loved and so wildly unselfconscious.

I still remember the enjoyment of that moment.
The transcendence of it. That experience is in me.
It will always be a part of me. Had it not occurred,
my life would in some way be diminished.
Even because of that seemingly trivial experience,
my life in some way has been enlarged.

It's something like that with God.

God experiences us,
and our experience is in God.
God feels, loves, hurts, hears, laughs, understands.
God is influenced by us.
The risk God takes in relating to us in love is real
and profound:
God's experience is diminished or enlarged by our
experience.

It's like when a mother cries because her child is hurting,
or when a close friend holds vigil at the hospital while
you're in surgery, or when you're so happy for someone
you feel that catch in your throat and get all gushy inside
and you can only force a few words out of your mouth
because you're over-the-top emotional.

This experience of God is best captured in the words of
the apostle Paul, who says, the "Spirit helps us in our
weakness ... *intercedes with groaning too deep for words.*"[14]

Breathing for us.
Breathing with us.
Groaning and sighing.
Taking us in.
Experiencing us in God's own self.

Does this change in any way how we experience
and relate to God?
How we respond to God's creative, relentless,
loving call on our lives?
How we see God experiencing and relating to the world?

As the poet William Blake once wrote in
The Marriage of Heaven and Hell, "Eternity is in love
with the productions of time."

PRESSED BETWEEN THE PAGES
OF MY MIND

Hirokazu Kore-eda's obscure but extraordinary film *After
Life*[15] is about a group of men and women who, having just
died, are ushered into an uninspiring halfway house. Each
is met by a counselor who kindly explains to them that
they are dead, that they will be here for a week, and that
their assignment is to choose one memory, one only, from
their lifetimes:

one memory they want to save for eternity.

That memory will be reconstructed and filmed in a studio.
At the end of the week, they will watch the film
and then move along to the afterlife, taking only that
memory with them.

They will spend eternity within their happiest memory.

The film is completely sober and unvarnished.
No special effects, no harps or angels, no Morgan
Freeman or Hallmark Channel religious sentimentality.
Just a cold, grey industrial building filled with twenty or so
dead people and a handful of staffers working on a very
tight deadline.

As the new guests try to pick their favorite memories,
they each struggle in various ways.
One worries that his memories aren't remarkable enough.
Another refuses to pick one at all.
Another is given seventy-one hours of video footage
of his life to watch to try to jog his memory.
One teenager picks a childhood memory of visiting

Disneyland and riding Splash Mountain, only to be told
that twenty-nine others before her have also chosen that
memory, and that maybe she should reconsider.

Each, eventually, chooses a memory:
a man remembers a wartime experience,
a woman remembers giving birth to a child,
a prostitute remembers a kind and tender client,
a teenager remembers resting in her mother's lap
as a young girl,
an elderly woman remembers the joy
of sitting under a shower of cherry blossoms.

What single memory would you chose
to take with you into eternity?

As the film unfolds, we learn that all the counselors
who work in this halfway house are only there because
they either refused or were unable to choose a memory
after they died. In a strange twist, one of them, Takashi—
a young man who died in war about fifty years earlier—
discovers a connection between himself and an elderly
new arrival. The new arrival, it turns out, had married
the fiancé Takashi left behind upon his untimely death.
After a long and unspectacular marriage, that woman
had also died.

Curious to learn what memory his former fiancé had taken
with her into eternity, Takashi pulls her film from storage
and watches. Her most cherished memory, he learns,
was of the two of them, just before he left for war, sitting
together on a park bench.

In discovering that he had figured in his fiancé's chosen
moment to cherish, Takashi comes to the realization that
"I have learned I was part of someone else's happiness."

When we breathe in the spirit of God together, we become
a part of one another's happiness.

When we breathe out our spirit, we become a part of God's happiness.

LET'S JUST BREATHE

When you hear the word *conspiracy*, what comes most immediately to mind for you?

Do you think of wild theories claiming that Elvis is still alive or that there is a secret military base in Nevada called "Area 51" or that there was a second gunman on the grassy knoll in Dallas when JFK was shot or that an alien spacecraft really did land on Dan Wilmot's farm in Roswell, New Mexico in 1947?

The phrase *to conspire* comes from the Latin *con*, meaning *together*, and *spirare*, meaning *breathe*.

To conspire means *to breathe together*.

The early church knew this. About fifty days after the death of Jesus, the book of Acts says the *Spirit* swept over a small group of followers who were huddled up in a house, hiding from the world. The *Spirit* didn't come to them like a gentle breeze. It came like a mighty wind that blew the roof off and swept over them and through them and in them.

Animated by the wind, they could breathe again. And once those breathless, frightened believers started breathing *together*, they found their courage to share the love and compassion of God with the world.

These once-timid disciples launched a conspiracy to change the world by
healing the sick,
feeding the hungry,
caring for widows and orphans,
forgiving, reconciling, redeeming, and baptizing.

Since ancient times, Christians have been praying the three-word breath prayer,
"Come, Holy Spirit."

In the ninth century, a German monk, Rabanus Maurus, wrote a song based on this breath prayer called *Veni Creator Spiritus*, or "Come, Creator Spirit."

By the thirteenth century, the prayer *Veni Sancte Spiritus*, or "Come, Holy Spirit," became a common prayer in the Western church, beginning with the powerful words,

> Come, Holy Spirit, fill the hearts of Thy faithful
> and enkindle in them the fire of Thy love.

Even today, Christians pray this simple line, *Come, Holy Spirit*, whenever they need guidance on what to do, or which way to go, or whenever they need courage to step out in faith, believing that they are breathing in, and breathing with, the Holy Spirit.

Come, Holy Spirit.

Breathing in,
breathing with,
breathing out the Spirit.

I thought of this at the end of my pilgrimage on the Camino, as I sat in the crowded Cathedral of Santiago de Compostela with hundreds of other malodorous pilgrims for one of the daily pilgrims' masses.

During the mass, the monks swing the *Botafumeiro*—a large ornate thurible of burning incense suspended from a pulley mechanism in the dome of the cathedral. In a tradition that dates back more than 1,000 years, when the monks pull the rope, the thurible swings back and forth and fills the entire nave with incense. The ritual goes on for several minutes—and it's mesmerizing.

I asked a local if this ritual has any religious meaning.

In halted English, he said, "Maybe. But I really think they do it because all the pilgrims stink so badly from their long journey that no one can breathe. When they finally swing the *Botafumeiro*, we can all stop holding our breath."

There is a God in the Bible many of us have never met—a God who is spirit and whose breath is everywhere.

This God is as near to us as our breath.

When we breathe,
this God is in us and we are in God.

When we breathe together,
we become part of the divine conspiracy.

Chapter 6

"bzzz"

the glory of god

What does it mean to be human, to be fully alive?

It's the question at the heart of the iconic film *Groundhog Day*,[1] about the narcissistic, Scrooge-like TV weatherman, Phil Connors, who is sent on a trivial assignment to cover the annual emergence of the groundhog—which predicts every February 2 whether it will be an early spring or six more weeks of winter.

While on assignment, Connors finds himself inexplicably stuck in a time loop, repeating the same day, over and over again—trapped in a place he loathes, surrounded by people he despises, given an assignment he detests, knowing that nothing he does can or will change his situation. He sinks into depression, succumbs to self-destructive behaviors and even loses his will to live.

In one unforgettable scene, Connors asks his friend, Ralph, "What would you do if you were stuck in one place and every day was exactly the same, and nothing you did mattered?"

Ralph says, "That about sums it up for me."

It's such a brilliant scene. And such a painful truth.

Ralph voices what many in the modern world fear most—
becoming a slave to routine,
stuck in endless drudgery,
trapped in a monotonous world with monochrome people,
living an unimaginative, inconsequential, meaningless life.

Meaning, purpose, beauty, mystery, novelty—
these are often the lamentable casualties of life
in the modern world.

And yet we know how absolutely vital they are
to being human.

What happened to them?

SOMEBODY THAT I USED TO KNOW

About 400 years ago, the Scientific Revolution taught
us how to break down the physical world into laws and
principles that could explain just about everything—
how things work,
why things happen,
what will happen based on what has already happened.

Four instruments revealed that the world is ordered
according to mechanistic, cause-and-effect laws—the
telescope, the microscope, the thermometer, and the
barometer.

All at once, we had an explanation for everything. Almost
nothing was a mystery anymore.

Why do earthquakes happen? There was a time when people would have blamed the Greek goddess Gaea for having a really bad day and stomping her foot on the ground.

But scientists could now resolve the mystery with two simple words: *tectonic plates.*

What about the tsunami that came immediately after the earthquake? It turned out it wasn't a Poseidon temper tantrum after all, as the Greeks once believed. It wasn't even an act of God, as the church had suggested. It was now easily explained by seismic activity, geologic uplift, wavelength, and gravity.

Science soon began to call into question everything we thought we knew and believed.

And that's when science and the church began to wonder if they could live together anymore. Their marriage had always been on the bubble. They'd only managed to stay together because, for centuries, they slept in separate beds and ate in separate rooms and took separate vacations.

But in the last third of the nineteenth century, Darwin theorized that humans were descended from apes. That's when both sides cited irreconcilable differences.

Science said to the church,
You just don't understand me.
You're suffocating me.
You're always on my back.
It's like I'm walking on eggshells all the time.
I can't live this way anymore.

And the church said,
Well allow me to retort.
It's you—you've changed.
You question every little thing I do or say.

You make me feel so incompetent and inadequate and old.
I don't even know who you are anymore.
I don't even know who we are anymore.

It ended in an ugly, public divorce. It was like Brad
and Jennifer. Or like Brad and Angelina. Only worse.
A lot of people died.

When the dust finally settled,
the church got to keep the cathedrals,
science kept the laboratories.

But the custody agreement created a lot of orphans in the
modern world.

Some people stayed with the church, but a growing
number of them no longer come home for weekend visits.

Many of those who do visit on weekends tend to blame
science for problems like
the decline of the so-called Christian nation,
atheism and agnosticism,
secular humanism and nihilism,
abortion and gender-neutralism,
the demise of moral values and the propagation of woke
indoctrination,
and almost anything and everything related to sex.

They tend to believe that science has caused more
problems than it has solved—
except for flush toilets and anesthesia and antibiotics,
of course.
And maybe Alexa. And The Clapper. And the Chia Pet.
And the Hot Pocket.

These have been useful.

Some people left the church and moved in with science
after the breakup. Many of them today reject religion
altogether.

They blame Christianity for atrocities like
the Crusades,
the Holocaust,
the trans-Atlantic slave trade,
homophobia, Islamophobia, sexism, white nationalism,
and a host of other social evils carried out
in the name of God.

They argue that Christianity is a system of
irrational,
oppressive,
archaic,
superstitious,
supernaturalistic,
supercalifragilistic magical thinking
that has no social benefit or cultural contribution
whatsoever—
except for some life-saving research hospitals.
And some great universities and rescue missions.
And maybe the Sistine Chapel, Handel's *Messiah*,
and the civil rights movement.

These, too, have been useful.

The modern world has convinced us that we must
pick a side because faith and science are incompatible,
irreconcilable, and only one of the two possesses the
truth.

Modernism, by the way, thrives on this kind of binary,
dichotomous, either/or, side-taking kind of thinking. It's
a convenient tool for blaming, scapegoating, villainizing,
otherizing, and categorizing groups of people into
buckets like—

Pro-life/Pro-choice
Coke/Pepsi
Conservative/Progressive
Chevy/Ford

Blue State/Red State
Body/Soul
Mac/PC
Science/Religion

If being right is your goal, binary thinking has its benefits.
Just pick a side and your question is resolved.

For those who have chosen to side with science,
the most pressing question tends to be,
how does it all work?

For those who have chosen to side with faith,
the most pressing question tends to be,
who makes it all work?

But what if our binary thinking has been leading us all
along to ask the wrong question?

What if our most urgent, burning question is not
how does it all work or
who makes it all work but
what does it mean to be human,
what does it mean to be fully alive?

Science can reveal the frequency of a G-flat and chart
the acoustic radiation patterns of mating calls in the
bird kingdom, but science cannot tell us why we find a
Beethoven symphony or the morning birdsong of the
nightingale so breathtakingly beautiful.

Science can tell us how our eyes relay information
about color to our brains and explain how light refracts
whenever its waves pass from one medium to another,
but science cannot tell us why gazing upon a Marc Chagall
painting or beholding the Milky Way on a clear night
broadsides us with awe and reverence and leaves us
speechless and starstruck.

Faith can give us words to explain the mystery and
transcendence of a God who created the earth and all that

is, but it does not give us any practical instructions for how to save the earth and the human race from climate disaster.

Faith can convince us to pray for our sick neighbor across the street or for victims of an earthquake half a world away, believing that we are all somehow wonderfully and mysteriously connected to each other, but faith doesn't have the language to explain how two subatomic particles traveling *away* from each other at the *speed of light*, to *opposite* ends of the universe, will remain *entangled*—even to the point that changing the electric charge of one particle will simultaneously change the charge of the other whether they are centimeters or millions of light years apart.

Both science and religion have betrayed us
in the modern world.
Both were determined only to be right.
Both failed to tell us what it means to be human
and most fully alive.
Both have operated for centuries from the same flawed understanding of what comprises the universe at its most basic level.

LET'S GET METAPHYSICAL

Metaphysics is the word we use to describe the study of reality and our understanding of the fundamental nature of reality. What are the most irreducible units of reality—the basic building blocks of the universe?

Take a moment right now and look around.
What do you see?

Chances are you see this book
you're holding in your hands,
the chair you're sitting on,

a table or desk,
a lamp,
a coffee cup, and
a Hot Pocket—because serious hunger
calls for a serious snack.

Maybe you see a pen or pencil,
a notepad,
some magazines,
a few books,
a cell phone.

What you likely *assume* you see are a handful of mostly
unrelated objects, all made up of matter. And matter,
we are told, is *the stuff that the universe is made of.*

But all matter consists of molecules. And molecules
are made up of atoms. And every high school chemistry
teacher will tell you that *the atom is the building block
of matter.*

I don't remember much more from Mr. Percy's high school
chemistry class, except that it's the type of atoms, and
the way in which atoms are arranged in a material, that
determines if that matter will have the properties of a
solid, liquid, or gas.

We've known about atoms for 2,500 years, thanks to
Democritus, who was the first to call these small pieces
of matter *atoms*, from the Greek word, *atomos*, meaning
indivisible. An atom, it was believed, is that which cannot
be broken down into smaller parts.

Which meant
the entire universe,
the ground beneath your feet,
the shoes on your feet,
the roof over your head,
the teeth in your head,
the hair on your head,

the blood circulating in your veins,
your heart, your brain, your lungs, your skin, your toenails,
your entire body and everybody
and every *body* around you—
it's all just a bunch of spiritless atoms bouncing around
like billiard balls,
atoms electronically attracted to other atoms and
arranged in a particular physical pattern and
joined together through a reaction called
chemical bonding.

Matter. Objects. Stuff. Things. Atoms.

Your body is an assembly of about seven octillion atoms.

But if this is what it means to be human, then being
human sounds lifeless, meaningless, spiritless.

Plato was one of the first to try to put some meaning back
into what it means to be human. He taught that body and
spirit are two different things. Plato said everything in the
physical world—what we see and experience in our daily
lives—is just a *representation* of ultimate or actual reality.
The physical world is full of tangible objects—
rocks,
chairs,
togas, and
human bodies
that are all merely imperfect representations of ideal
Forms that exists in a spiritual realm, which he called
the *Realm of Forms*. A *Form* was an aspatial (outside of
space), atemporal (outside of time) blueprint of perfection
that existed only in the *Realm of Forms*.

In other words, everything you see in the physical world
is imperfect and inferior to the ideal, which can only be
found in a realm outside of space, beyond time. Every
physical object in this world, while imperfect, reflects to
some degree the glory of the ideal it represents.

To make sense of Plato's metaphysics, try this:

Draw a triangle on a piece of paper. I'm going to guess that your triangle isn't perfect: its lines might not be completely straight; its angles probably do not line up to exactly 180 degrees.

Draw another triangle and that one won't be perfect either—because it's virtually impossible to draw a *perfect* triangle.

Nonetheless, it's probably recognizable as a triangle. Show it to someone. Ask them if it looks like a triangle. If they say it looks like a circle, you've got bigger issues.

Plato argued that your triangle isn't a *real* triangle. It's simply a *representation* of the ideal triangle form that exists in the *Realm of Forms*.

Why does this matter?

Plato's metaphysics elevated spiritual things over physical things by suggesting that the *only* things that are real and of inherent value are *outside* of time and space. Spirit, according to Plato, is *more* real and *more* worthy than anything that can be found in the physical, imperfect world.

This marked a fundamental shift in how we see God. According to Plato, one of the perfect *Forms* was the Divine form, which implied that God is outside of time and space—a concept completely foreign to the Hebrew mindset and the biblical canon. Christian theologians like Augustine and Aquinas, and many who came later, subsequently built their entire theological systems on Plato's metaphysics, out of which emerged unbiblical concepts of an other-worldly God with attributes like omnipotence, omniscience, and immutability.

But Plato's metaphysics also marked a major shift in how we see the world around us.

The physical world,
all living things,
all the material things we find beautiful,
all the people around us,
the human bodies we all live our lives in—
these were now suddenly seen as less than real,
less than ideal,
of lesser value.

And because how we see the world determines how we
act toward the world, this body/spirit dualistic thinking can
have serious consequences.
Anything or anyone we perceive as less than real
will be given less than real love and
less than real concern and
less than real commitment and real value.

Plato's student, Aristotle, took his teacher's thought one
step further. Things in the physical world, said Aristotle,
are not representations of *Forms,* but *substances.* The word
substance corresponds to the Greek word *ousia,* which
means *being*—later transmitted via the Latin *substantia,*
which means *something that stands under or grounds things.*

Being, said Aristotle, is *substance or thingness.* What exists,
exists as an object—a thing with specific qualities and
well-defined spatial and temporal limits. For example:
Harley is my dog. He's an Australian shepherd. He has
blue eyes. He is seven years old.

Aristotle said that to understand my dog Harley, or
anything in reality, we can only focus on what actually is—
substances, things, matter.

And what is matter made of?

Atoms. Lots and lots of atoms.

Aristotle's metaphysics gave rise to our dominant modern
worldview in which reality is conceived as an assembly of

static components called atoms and there's no divine hum or spirit pulsing through us and God cannot be known or experienced in this actual world because God, standing *outside* of time and space, is not an actual substance. God is just the *Prime Mover* and *Unmoved Mover* of the universe who, from outside the cosmos,
got all of this started,
made all of this happen,
and has remained uninvolved in all of this ever since.

Aristotle's metaphysics, like Plato's, laid the foundation for many unbiblical, intractable Christian doctrines that turned God into an all-powerful, all-knowing, unchanging, and timeless heavenly being who watches over us from a distance.

CHECK OUT THE BIG BRAIN ON BRAD

There was one more major development that shaped our modern worldview. It led to the ugly divorce between science and the church we talked about earlier. It's known as the Scientific Revolution.

All those instruments we had invented for observing and analyzing and predicting and calibrating our physical world turned out to be extremely useful. They contributed to some remarkable discoveries and innovations that opened up a whole new world for us.

We could suddenly *see* everything in the physical world, even things we couldn't actually see with our eyes—
stars and planets and
light waves and sound waves and
speed and motion and
cells and bacteria and amoeba and
protons and electrons and neutrons and elements and

gravity and electricity and fields and currents and
atmospheric pressure and temperature and
molecules and
lots and lots and lots of atoms.

It seemed to confirm everything that Aristotle had told us
centuries before: it's all *substance*.

What we couldn't see or measure or analyze with any
of those clever instruments was considered spiritual.
There was no way to prove the Bible's claims of a divine
presence pulsing through this world, or the inexplicable
healings and miracles of Jesus, or the strange hums
and nudges and woos and hints of providence or
transcendence we felt—all the spirit and soul stuff that the
Bible said was ultimate reality and the ground of being.

Everything that was thought to be real was reduced to
cogs and wheels and pullies and turbines and levers and
order and probability and laws and theorems and
matter and molecules and lots and lots of lifeless atoms,
all holding up the enormous weight of a soulless,
substance-based world.

And just as the modern squeegee known as the scientific
method wrung out the final drops of mystery and spirit
and soul from our theological imaginations, a philosopher,
René Descartes, sucked the oxygen out of the *substance* of
the world with his famous line, *Cogito, ergo sum.*

I think, therefore I am.

It seems like such an innocuous statement today. But
before this groundbreaking philosophical innovation, even
as science disputed all things spiritual, people of faith
could still say with some degree of authority that God had
spoken to them—that they had in some way *experienced*
God. They couldn't prove it scientifically, but they could
still claim it as their indisputable truth.

But Descartes argued that the only way we can know that *anything* is true—even truth itself—is not because God chose to *reveal* it to us, but because we *deduced* it through our own logic and thinking.

Descartes insisted that nothing that is *perceived* or *sensed—not even the human body—*is necessarily true or certain and therefore can never be trusted.

Like Plato, Descartes dismissed the inherent value of the body and the material world.
Like Aristotle, he affirmed that the world is made up solely of substances.

But, said Descartes, there are *two* kinds of substances: there is material body, or *matter*, of which the essential property is that it is *spatially extended*;
and there is mental substance, or *mind*, of which the essential property is that it *thinks*.

Because matter can't be trusted, it's inferior to the mind. Which means that the fundamental building block of reality, according to Descartes, is the *mind*.

He famously wrote,

> I thence concluded that I was a substance whose whole essence or nature consists only in thinking, and which, that it may exist, has need of no place, nor is dependent on any material thing.[2]

And with that revolutionary philosophical invention, our modern worldview was made complete and airtight. The world is made up of matter and mind. Matter is inherently flawed, so the only way we can truly know what we know to be true is through our thinking and reasoning.

Descartes's thought continues to impact our modern world today. By placing ultimate value on human reason, many moderns have gradually come to the now pervasive assumption that we can't trust divine revelation. Descartes was a devout Christian but, ironically, he helped lay the foundation for modern atheism, which sees faith and reason as incompatible, and truth as discovered only by thinking. This, for atheists, makes God unnecessary.

But perhaps more importantly, Descartes' view of *mind over matter*, otherwise known as Cartesian dualism, has led to some serious problems with how we see the human body, the material world, and creation itself.

It's given rise to the modern Christian emphasis on salvation as purely personal and spiritual while dismissing the communal, social, and global implications of God's ongoing redemptive work in the world.

It's led to some odd and deeply unbiblical concepts—like the so-called *rapture* that's perceived by some Christians as a spiritual escape plan from the physical world.

And the popular notion that the body is just a shell or temporary vessel for the soul.

And the common assumption that planet Earth has been given to us to dominate and dispose of by God, who may or may not restore it after the apocalypse.

When matter doesn't matter, we tend to
objectify it,
abuse it,
destroy it,
ignore it,
abandon it.

Plato, Aristotle, and Descartes, along with a host of other influential thinkers, have shaped over time—
how we see and interact with the world,
how we read the Bible,
how we perceive space and time,

how we believe what is and isn't believable,
and what we believe it means to be human.

Their thought gave rise to our modern worldview, which
suggests that being fully human means finding our place
in the great machine of a spiritless universe, riding on the
back of this lonely, rogue rock called Earth where, for a
handful of decades, we can make meaning by
pulling some levers,
pushing some buttons,
moving around some wheels and pullies—
making sure we don't get stuck in between the cogs
and trying to enjoy ourselves while we can
because what we see is all there is.

Just lots and lots of atoms.

But then something happened quite unexpectedly. One
of our nifty scientific instruments revealed something
mysterious inside all those atoms that we had never
seen before.

Lots and lots and lots of ... *quarks.*

It turns out there's a lot more than matter and mind.

There's *energy.*

And energy, we now know,
is the most irreducible unit of reality—
the basic building block of the universe.

And energy is everywhere.

GOOD TO THE LAST DROP

In the early 1900s, the French scientist and Jesuit priest
Pierre Teilhard de Chardin transcended the binary thinking
that led to the split between science and faith. He rejected

the dualism of mind/matter, body/soul, substance/spirit that dominated modern metaphysics.

As a paleontologist and theologian, when de Chardin observed the world, he perceived an intimate connection between the spiritual and material. In claiming that all physical matter in the universe was infused with divine presence, de Chardin was one of the first to attempt to reconcile faith and science, helping to shape a new way of perceiving our world that didn't require us to separate matter from spirit, body from soul.

He said the whole universe—even in all its imperfection—is suffused with the sacred, with a divine energy that animates everything.

You've probably seen one of de Chardin's most famous lines—the one emblazoned on T-shirts and bumper stickers that says,

> We are not human beings having a spiritual experience; we are spiritual beings having a human experience.

Right around the same time, the British mathematician-philosopher Alfred North Whitehead was also thinking about metaphysics. He wrote a magnum opus called *Process and Reality* that is pretty much incomprehensible without some serious explanation and some magic mushrooms. In it, he, like de Chardin, rejected the substance-based worldview. He said that the final real things—the fundamental units of reality—are not substances,
but occasions,
events,
drops of experience.

Every *occasion* is partially determined by every previous occasion, but always has an element of choice, however trivial. Every occasion, from you in this moment to the occasions that make up your body, to those that make up rocks and chairs and Hot Pockets and universes, have a subjective experience—though this experience is only conscious in humans and perhaps some animals. When you choose what to become in this instant from the possibilities available, you participate in the coming-to-be, or the process of becoming, of all future occasions—especially the one that is yourself in the next moment. To paraphrase Whitehead, *you are what the universe is for you, including your own reaction.*

Whitehead's thoughts opened a whole new way of seeing the world, and a whole new way of thinking about God.

First, he demonstrated that
everything impacts everything else in the universe.
The universe is fundamentally relational.
In every moment, you—and every other being
in the universe—
inherit everything that has ever
happened in the past and
then choose how you will express
what you are beyond yourself.
"The many become one and are increased by one,"
Whitehead famously wrote.

Second, he showed how
things that *look* like matter
are actually events or subjective experiences,
and things that *seem* like individual entities
are actually *societies* of subjective experiences.

Think of your body—your liver, lungs, blood cells and enzymes and hormones and the 1,000 different species of microbes crawling around on your skin right now. Each of these are their own individual occasion within the larger *society* of occasions that is you.

On a macro scale, that means the universe is not only *relational*, it's also *experiential*—all the way down to the lowest forms of life.

Which leads to another of Whitehead's big breakthroughs—that every real thing in the entire universe, whether conscious or not, has some element of subjective experience and some degree of individual freedom, however trivial. Even rocks and Hot Pockets. This doesn't mean they have *consciousness*. But it does mean they have some inherent and intrinsic value. To paraphrase Whitehead, *consciousness presupposes experience, not experience consciousness.*

Where is God in all of this?

God, suggested Whitehead, is also an occasion, an event of subjective experience. This shouldn't really come as a shock, even to the most orthodox believer, because most would agree that God doesn't have an actual physical body—at least not a human body.

As an occasion,
God is the source of creativity in the universe.
God conceives of all the possibilities for every occasion, like you and me, and
gives each occasion an aim or impulse
toward the highest relevant possibility in the mind of God.
In our own process of becoming, we choose how closely to actualize that aim.
This means that we are free, that our future is open.
It means that God is present to every occasion in the universe in every moment.
God feels, receives, is influenced by, and integrates the consequence of every creaturely choice into God's own self,
and therefore, seeks to enrich God's own experience by enriching the experience of everyone and everything.
Whitehead called this enriched experience *zestiness*.

I love that word.

Zestiness.

Try to say *zestiness* without smiling.

Whitehead gave us a new way of understanding and
experiencing God—a way that's profoundly consistent with
how the ancient Hebrews and early Christians conceived
of and experienced God—one who is—
all-loving,
ever-present,
immanent,
creative,
responsive,
unchanging but ever-changing.

A God who does not stand outside of space and time.
A God who knows and feels what it's like to be human.
A God whose deepest desire is to help us humans be
most fully human and most fully alive.

NOW THIS IS GETTING WEIRD

What does it mean to be human?

The human body is a remarkably elegant
and complex network of

7 octillion atoms and
35-40 trillion cells and
700 enzymes and
206 bones
all connected by tendons, ligaments, and cartilage and
powered by 6 quarts of blood that
pump through 60,000 miles of blood vessels
at a pace of 100,000 heartbeats per day,
all managed by brain impulses traveling across 45 miles of
nerve pathways

at a speed of 200,000 mph,
all held together by 22 square feet of skin
less than .5mm thick.

The human body is a brilliant, breathtaking work of engineering. But is this what it means to be human?

Not completely.

Because the human body, like the universe itself, is 99.9 percent empty space.

The nucleus of an atom is virtually 100 percent of the entire atom's mass. If you were to enlarge a single atom to, say, 500 square feet, the size of the nucleus would still be like a speck of dust. The space between it and the outer band of electrons is merely empty space.

You, me, our bodies, our highly sophisticated brains, are 99.9 percent empty space. Remember this next time someone calls you an airhead. Technically speaking, they're right.

So what's happening in all that empty space in us, in the universe?

Not long after de Chardin and Whitehead were imagining new ways to understand God and the world, quantum physicists found previously undiscovered subatomic particles in an entire physical world of their own deep within the nucleus. They're known as *quarks*—the smallest of all known particles of all physical matter, mathematically understood to contain a near empty void of vibrating waves of light energy that physicists refer to as *strings*. It's now understood that the frequency, or vibration, of these subatomic waves of energy will determine the various materials, like air, water, wood, steel, or Hot Pockets, that we observe from our physical, three-dimensional perspective.

Quarks are funky. They're not all the same. They come in six *flavors*, representing their differences in mass and charge and spin: *up, down, top, bottom, strange, and charm.*

But regardless of their flavor, all quarks behave weirdly. They can change flavors—*down* quarks can turn into *up* quarks and *charm* quarks into *strange* quarks.
Some quarks exist and then disappear for reasons we can't explain.
Some quarks disappear the instant we observe them— proving that our observation of reality, presumed to be *objective*, exerts influences on reality that we cannot explain.
Some quarks disappear over here and then reappear over there—without even traveling the distance between them.

But all quarks seem to exist in combination with other quarks. They're highly *social, relational* entities. Quarks don't exist apart from other quarks. And when you put a bunch of quarks together, you get one funky, quirky, quarky party.

Which partly explains their weirdest behavior of all: quarks that at one time shared the same identical state— the same system of coordinates—remain instantly and enduringly connected.
Under certain conditions they are so thoroughly *entangled* with each other that they're not just here or there, but in all measured places at the same time.
Their nonlocality respects neither time nor space: it exists whether the distance that separates them is measured in millimeters or in light-years, and whether the time that separates them consists of seconds or of millions of years.

Are you following this?

At first, we thought the universe was made up of atoms.
Then we learned that atoms were 99.9 percent
empty space.
And now we know that all that space in all those atoms—
in the entire universe—isn't 99.9 percent *empty*.

It's 99.9 percent *energy*.

And so are we. At the very heart of the universe is a deep,
inherent, irrefutable, inexplicable longing for relationship.

In each of our bodies,
there are fifty-quadrillion coordinated biochemical events
taking place at this very moment. Every second, each
of our 30-40 trillion cells is generating fifty thousand
biochemical events
in an almost perfectly coordinated dance of atoms and
molecules that make possible everything from voluntary
movement
to the continuous complex processes of
circulation, digestion, assimilation, elimination, respiration,
growth, and healing.

The physical body is the manifestation of an energy field
made of dynamic spaces of vibration.
Nothing ever rests.
Everything continually vibrates.
Everything, in some subtle way, is always moving.
Every living thing pulses with the flow of life force that
pervades the universe.
Life is movement.
Everything in the universe is composed of relationships
of energy.

What de Chardin, Whitehead, and now quantum physicists
have been trying to tell us is we're not lifeless, spiritless
atoms all bouncing off each other after all. We're
ensouled bodies,

embodied souls
humming with divine spirit,
entangled with one another,
caught up in a dance of unimaginable beauty and
unmitigated energy.

The whole universe is composed of little strings of energy,
all vibrating in relationship to each other.

An ancient songwriter knew this long before metaphysics
and quantum physics—

> The heavens are telling the glory of God,
>   and the firmament proclaims his handiwork.
> Day to day pours forth speech,
>   and night to night declares knowledge.
> There is no speech, nor are there words;
>   their voice is not heard;
> yet their voice[strings][3] goes out through all the earth
>   and their words to the end of the world.[4]

Divine entanglement,
energy everywhere,
in all living things,
uniting all living things.

The apostle Paul was right. Nothing in heaven or on earth
can separate us from the love of God.[5]

This is what it means to be alive.
Ensouled bodies,
embodied souls,
spirit and matter,
entangled with God.

Jesus didn't need quantum physics to prove this. He
already understood that spirit and matter are inseparable.
And to be fully human and alive, both need to dance.

There's a story from Luke about the day Jesus was home
in Capernaum and some Pharisees and scribes and

followers came from miles away to hear him teach. The house was packed with so many people that the large crowd had spilled out the doorway and into the yard.

While Jesus is teaching, four men arrive, carrying their disabled friend on a pallet. They hope Jesus might heal their friend. But there's no way into the house through the crowd.

So they get creative, hoisting their friend onto the roof of the house.

In the first century, a roof was made of wooden beams stretching from wall to wall. It was topped with a mat of reeds and clay. Sand and stones were then rolled into the clay, sealing it from the weather.

Can you see this scene in your mind?

Jesus is teaching to a packed house.
The crowd is sitting in silence,
hanging on every word of Jesus.
And in the middle of the sermon,
small flakes of reed and clay begin drifting down,
falling from the sky—
first just a dusting,
then a shower of debris,
then a flood of sunlight filling the room,
then a human body,
slowly descending.

It would almost be comical if it weren't so beautiful.

A hole in the roof.
A crippled man on a pallet.
Four faces looking down from above on the crowd below.

It's a strange story. In fact, it ends with the people saying, *"We have seen strange things today."*[6]

But there are two insights from this story that are so relevant to what it means to be human, to be alive in the modern world.

The first is that we are only as well as the community to which we belong.

The man on the pallet is a *paralytic*. The Greek word suggests palsy, a nervous system disorder. But his entire community has made it impossible for him to be well, to be fully alive.

Unable to walk, he can't be an active member of his community. He's confined to a life of isolation and complete dependence on others. He's hidden from the world. He's labeled as an *other*.

And because his religion associates his disability with sin, he's marked by shame and stigma and excluded from the temple. The priests said, "Palsy doesn't just happen. There must be a spiritual explanation for your condition."

The man is entrapped by societal and religious systems that make him sick and keep him sick.

We are all subjects in an ecosystem. In a world that perceives reality as just a bunch of atoms, we assume we can observe the world objectively, as though we are outside the system, "above place." But we are unmistakably influenced by the places and communities in which we live, by our relationships in and to those places. We're inseparable from the relational fields in which we find ourselves.

Which is why we ask people, "So, where are you from?"

Place, people, geography, and tribe tell us a lot about a person.

I read about children suffering from strange cancers and diseases along the shores of the Horn of Africa. European companies had dumped barrels of nuclear waste into the ocean in that region for decades. When the December 2011 tsunami struck the coast, those long-forgotten barrels dislodged and broke open, spilling uranium, mercury, and lead across the seabed, contaminating the local food source for thousands of miles.

We are only as well as the community to which we belong, which makes the dumping of toxic waste a deeply spiritual issue.

I was recently in conversations with community leaders and public health professionals about the well-being of the youth and young adults in my county. Why, we asked, do our young people report lower levels of emotional well-being and resilience, higher levels of anxiety and depression, and account for higher incidents of suicide relative to national averages? Is there something in the water we're all swimming in?

Is it just bad atoms?

Here's something that keeps me up at night—
I'm a pastor to a mother whose son was a school shooter.
I'm a pastor to a young victim of a school shooting—*in a separate incident.*
I'm a pastor to schoolteachers, counselors, and students who survived the shooting at Columbine High School.
I'm a pastor to first responders who treated victims of the Aurora theater shooting.

All these tragedies occurred within a 10-mile radius of my church.

Our modern worldview tells us it's just some bad atoms.
Just get rid of the bad atoms.
Swap out the bad ones for good ones and everything will be OK.

But it's not the atoms. It's the relationships between them.

THE SHIP OF THESEUS

The ancient Greeks devised a thought experiment,
a puzzle, called "the ship of Theseus."

Theseus was a mythical king who had lots of cool
adventures at sea. When Theseus returned from all his
sea-faring adventures, his ship was preserved by the
Athenians for centuries. As you might imagine, the ship
began to deteriorate from all that coastal weather and
ocean air. Over time, each plank of the ship's hull was
replaced when it started to rot—one by one, over many
years—until eventually, not even one of the original
planks was left.

The paradox of Theseus's ship raised the question—

If you're replacing parts of Theseus's ship, at what point
does the ship cease to be Theseus's ship?

Some argued that when even one plank of the ship is
replaced, it's no longer Theseus's ship.
Others said that regardless of how many boards are
replaced, it's aways Theseus's ship.
The philosopher Thomas Hobbes later asked: what if,
when the rotten planks were replaced, some wise guy had
taken all the old, rotten ones, preserved them, and then
reused them to build *another* ship and called *it* Theseus's
ship? Which ship would be the real one?

But if they'd asked Jesus how to solve the paradox of
Theseus's ship, he'd say this: it's not really about the
planks. Some may be rotten and need replacing. But
planks don't make a ship. Planks don't make a ship float.

It's how the planks relate to all the other planks that
makes it a ship.
It's about the relationships that hold the planks together
and make the whole ship float.

We're only as well as the relationships we share with those in the communities to which we belong. We can't just replace bad atoms with good atoms and expect *shalom*.

Years ago, some pastors from the Denver metro area got together to think about how their churches could better serve their communities. They invited the mayor to a meeting, and asked him a simple question—

How can we best work together to serve our city?

The pastors identified a long list of social problems: at-risk kids, substandard housing, child hunger, substance abuse, mental illness. After listening to these pastors list all the problems that needed to be addressed, the mayor gave them an astonishingly simple solution. He said most of the issues our community is facing would be eliminated or drastically reduced if we could just figure out a way to become a community of great neighbors.

He said that often when people identify a social problem, they come to civic officials and say, "This is a serious issue, and you should start a program to address it."

But the mayor suggested that perhaps programs aren't always the most effective way to address social issues. Maybe *relationships* are a more powerful force for real social change. He said that when neighbors actually have relationships with one another,
the elderly shut-in gets looked after by the person next door,
the at-risk child gets mentored by a dad
who lives on the block,
the dilapidated house on the corner gets repaired
by caring neighbors,
crime rates drop and
people live longer and healthier and happier lives.[7]

Isn't that ironic? A group of pastors asks the mayor how they can best serve their city, and the mayor tells them that the best solution is to get the people in their churches to practice the second half of the Great Commandment:

Love your neighbor as yourself.[8]

Which is why those four men in the story, driven by love, tear a hole in a roof to get their friend the help he needs.

Because they are well, they can make him well.

Darius Goes West[9] is a little-known but poignant film that documents the true story of a group of friends, one of whom, Darius, has Duchenne muscular dystrophy and has lost his mobility. He's fifteen years old.

After learning that Darius has never left his little town in Georgia, his friends take him on a 7,000-mile road trip in an RV across the United States to California. Their mission is to get the hit MTV show *Pimp My Ride* to pimp his electric wheelchair. Along the way, they take him on a swamp boat ride in New Orleans, a river rafting trip on the Colorado River, a tour of Las Vegas, and a hot air balloon ride in Temecula, California.

Eventually, they arrive at the Pacific Ocean, where they wheel him through the sand into the water and lift him up so he can stand in the ocean for the first time and feel the waves crash over his body. He laughs uncontrollably while his friends hold him under his arms so that his feet can dangle against the sand.

It's a story about how we are only as well as the communities to which we belong. This is what it means to be human and fully alive.

Who are you tearing the roof off for?

A BODY IN A SOUL

One other insight from the Luke story is that physical wellness is a spiritual matter.

Today we know that so much of our physical illness is of a deeper, spiritual origin. We have a word for this relationship: *psychosomatic*, from two Greek words: *psuche*, meaning *mind/soul*; and *somatikos*, meaning *body*. Our feelings, emotions, memories, and conscience play a central role on the human illness-wellness continuum.

There are no bodies and souls. There are only ensouled bodies, embodied souls. Spirit and matter are entangled. Whenever our spirit aches or suffers abuse, trauma, exhaustion, or pain, it uses material form—our physical body—to tell us.

Addiction.
Bulimia.
Cutting.
Overwork.
Insomnia.
Hypertension.

Whenever there is ache or emptiness of spirit,
our physical bodies tell the truth.

Likewise, whenever our bodies suffer trauma, exhaustion, or pain, our souls shout out, call out, cry out to us.

Depression.
Anxiety.
Anger.
Fear.
Worry.
Suspicion.
Hopelessness.

Not every physical illness is of a spiritual origin.
But nearly every spiritual injury or emotional trauma has
the capacity to manifest itself in profoundly physical ways.

We are the sum of our past.
We are societies of experience.

Our bodies tell us if we're anxious,
fearful,
stressed,
exhausted or
content,
at peace,
happy or
rested.

This information is transmitted through
physical signals like
perspiration,
respiration,
heart rate,
headaches,
back pain,
blood pressure.

Our bodies tell us how our lives really are and whether
we are truly well. Our bodies are often the only prophets
that can speak truthfully when we are otherwise unable or
unwilling to listen to ourselves or others.

Which is why, when the man is dropped at the feet
of Jesus, seeking to be healed of his physical disability,
Jesus first offers him spiritual healing.

Your sins are forgiven, Jesus tells the man.

Does this sound like an odd, perhaps even cruel,
thing to say to someone in his condition?

The man comes to Jesus for bodily restoration,
but Jesus first heals spirit because to restore his
physical health without restoring spirit would be
to ignore the much deeper tragedy of
living a life devoid of meaning and purpose and
beauty and community.

Your sins are forgiven.

Jesus isn't talking about the man's personal
transgressions. He's pronouncing release and liberation
from all those labels and limitations placed upon him by
his community, all the conventions that have marked him
as other than, less than, different than, all the dogmas that
have robbed him of spirit.

This is the real nature of sin.

Sin is the impoverishment or diminishment or
impairment[10] of our relationships with God, with ourselves,
with others, and with creation. *Sin*, from the Greek,
hamartia, has its origins not in any theological or spiritual
context, but in the ancient Greek sport of archery.
Hamartia means *to miss the mark or bullseye*. Sometimes
you draw the bowstring, set your aim, release the arrow,
and you miss the mark.

Individuals can *miss the mark*.
So, too, can whole communities and societies.

Sin is the word we use to describe how our beliefs
and patterns of behavior, or those of others or even of
systems acting upon us, miss the mark and perpetuate
relational impoverishment or diminishment that leads to
un-peace—what theologian Cornelius Plantinga calls the
"culpable disturbance of shalom."

Your sin is forgiven, says Jesus to the man
who fell through the roof.
You're free now to be fully alive.

Maybe this is what Irenaeus, the early church theologian, meant when he said *the glory of God is a human being fully alive.*

How free are you to be fully alive and fully at peace? Is there any impediment, impairment, disturbance that keeps your body-soul from dancing together with God and the world?

YOU JUST HAD A NEAR-LIFE EXPERIENCE

John Wesley, an Anglican priest in the late eighteenth century, devised some questions for people to use in what he called class meetings. Today, we might call them small groups.
Ordinary people would gather in these groups, and they'd talk through some very personal questions, such as:

> Am I consciously or unconsciously creating the impression that I am better than I am?
> Am I honest in all my acts and words, or do I exaggerate?
> Am I self-conscious, self-pitying, or self-justifying?
> Am I a slave to dress, friends, work, or habits?
> Am I jealous, impure, critical, irritable, touchy, or distrustful?
> Is there anyone whom I fear, dislike, disown, criticize, hold resentment toward, or disregard?
> Do I insist upon doing something about which my conscience is uneasy?
> Am I defeated in any part of my life?

There were 22 questions in all, each getting to the heart of what it means to be human, to find purpose, meaning, beauty, wonder, in that intimate, unmitigated dance between your body-spirit and God's.

What does it mean to be human, to be fully alive?

It starts with understanding that we are neither bodies
nor souls but
embodied souls, ensouled bodies,
who are only as well as the relationships we share
with all the embodied souls and ensouled bodies
around us.

Chapter 7

"owh"

the salvation of god

When I was fifteen, a friend invited me to his church one summer night for a "crusade." While I didn't exactly understand what a crusade was, my friend assured me that there would be free pizza and Orange Crush after the show.

And that was all he had to say.

On the way to the crusade, my friend's father said to me in a *Oh, by the way, did-we-mention* kind of move, that there might be an altar call at the end of the night and, if I felt *convicted by the Spirit*, I could give my life to the Lord.

I told my friend's father that I had been a Catholic for a long time and that I'd just started going to a Methodist church so I was pretty sure I had all my bases covered and that things were good between me and the Lord, but can I still have the free pizza?

The crusade involved a lot of singing, led by a very cool rock band that sang songs that almost sounded like songs I had heard on the radio. But the main event featured a group of Christian evangelistic body builders called *The Power Team*—about a dozen ripped dudes dressed in muscle tees and Lycra shorts three sizes too small.

The members of *The Power Team* marched out flashing their chiseled forearms and six-pack abs while pulling giant refrigerators across the stage with their bleached-white teeth. They busted planks of wood and concrete blocks with their massive foreheads and tore license plates in half with their bare hands—*license plates!*

All in the name of Jesus.

The whole show was a staggering combination of impressive and weird. I didn't understand what Jesus had to do with tearing a phone book in half or breaking a baseball bat over your leg. But they were extraordinary athletes, and in between tricks they gave testimonies about how Jesus had saved them and how, at the end of tonight's show, Jesus could save me too.

The show lasted about an hour. And when the altar call was given, my friend looked at me like, *Well? Eh?*

I didn't get saved that night.
I've still never gotten saved.

I know many who have, and for a lot of them, it seems to have been life changing. I know people who, having experienced a particular, decisive encounter with God's grace and forgiveness, found peace, purpose, sobriety, reconciliation with others, a second chance, or a fresh start in life.

For many of them, salvation signifies redemption, deliverance, rescue, eternal life, and getting into heaven. And it often involves specific steps—

saying a special prayer and
believing in the atoning act of Jesus' death on the
    cross and
confessing Jesus as Lord and Savior and
trusting that when they die, they will go to heaven.

It can be an effective and efficient transaction, which explains why highly trained associates of Jesus approach us in public places like supermarket parking lots with Gospel tracts asking us if we are saved. While we're just swinging by to pick up a loaf of bread and some Slim Jims, they're reminding us that we're going to die, that it could happen tonight, and that we better have an eternal life insurance policy.

Maybe this is why, when some people hear the word *salvation*, they think of Christianity as a cringe-and-fringe religion and reject it altogether. They struggle with this false but popular and highly profitable message that the next life is more important than the one they're living today, or that *heaven*, which we cannot see, is more important to God than the earthly world we can see.

Some people cannot reconcile that kind of God with their real, lived experience. They struggle to live in this dual reality in which
matter and spirit,
body and soul,
earth and heaven,
the human and divine,
this age and the age to come
must be separated and ordered hierarchically.

If you've ever been disillusioned by this Christian dualism that suggests that God only cares about the salvation of our souls, I assure you that the God of the Bible is one who is always working to bring these apparent opposites together.

This God cares so deeply, even ultimately,
about earthly things
that the Word became flesh and lived among us.[1]

Christians make the radical claim that this
Word-became-flesh God had
a real name and
a real birthplace and
a real body and
a real childhood and
a real death.

He didn't walk the streets of Galilee with a halo
on his head, as if he were *not of this world*.

He was the embodied soul, the ensouled body,
of the divine.

He cared a lot about human things—
human problems,
human relationships,
human bodies,
human suffering,
human injustice,
human joy,
human flourishing,
human freedom.

He also cared deeply about things
we tend to call *spiritual*—
devotion to God,
prayer,
Torah,
Sabbath rest,
generosity,
how not to gain the whole world but lose our souls.[2]

Jesus cared so deeply about human things and
spiritual things that he taught that
human things are spiritual things and

spiritual things are human things,
and that there is no fixed boundary that separates
body from soul,
flesh from spirit,
earth from heaven,
this life from the next life.

THIS IS ME

One day, soon after moving out of his parents' basement
and spending some time alone in the wilderness, Jesus
comes back home to Nazareth. He's about thirty years
old, and he's in a bit of transitional period, having just
been baptized by a fiery prophet and close family relative
named John.

Jesus is coming to terms with the serious ball of God wax
that is his life and calling, so he stops by the synagogue
on the Sabbath. The synagogue leader notices that Jesus
is *full of the Holy Spirit*, so he invites Jesus to give the
sermon.

When he hands Jesus the scroll containing the words of
the prophet Isaiah, Jesus unrolls it and reads these words:

> "The Spirit of the Lord is upon me,
>   because he has anointed me
>   to bring good news to the poor.
> He has sent me to proclaim release to the captives
>   and recovery of sight to the blind,
>   to set free those who are oppressed,
> to proclaim the year of the Lord's favor."[3]

Everyone in the synagogue that day knows this passage.
It's the prophecy of the long-awaited messiah who will
someday come to bring salvation to the people of Israel.

As Jesus reads this familiar passage,
the people are nodding their heads.
That's our boy, Jesus, all grown up, someone says.
I remember when he used to ride his scooter in the
cul-de-sac as a child, says another, and now look at him,
so faithful, reading about what the messiah will do
when he finally comes.

But then, all at once, Jesus stops reading. He rolls up the
Isaiah scroll and says the most unexpected thing—the one
thing that will change how everything that ever comes
after this one thing will be heard.

"Today," says Jesus, "this scripture has been fulfilled
in your hearing."[4]

It's his first sermon. His inauguration speech.
And what he's saying is—
I am Messiah. The one about whom I have just read ...
is me.

In that moment in the synagogue, Jesus didn't just unroll
the scroll of Isaiah and read a few verses.

In this decisive moment, Jesus has just unrolled the scroll
of his very life and read what the next chapter of his story
would be all about.

What he is saying is—
This is me.
This is who I am.
This is what I have come to do.

Did you notice what is and isn't on the Messiah's
to-do list?

First, notice what's *not* on the list: anything that, in the
modern world, we would call even remotely *spiritual*.

He doesn't say, I have come that you might
receive me into your heart.

He doesn't say, I have come that you might
have a personal relationship with me.

He doesn't even say, I have come to save you from your
personal sins.

Did you know that Jesus never once actually said these
things—*anywhere*? Jesus never used this transactional
language when he spoke of his mission.

I have no doubt Jesus was in the hearts of a lot of people.
He clearly was all about having personal relationships.
He often exercised an unusual power to heal and release
people from personal sin.

These, we know, were important to Jesus. But in his very
first sermon in which he announces his life purpose and
divine calling, none of them are at the top of his to-do list.

Did you notice what *is* on the to-do list for Jesus?

It's all profoundly human stuff—down-to-earth, messy,
fleshy, real-world human stuff.

To preach good news to the poor, he says.
Not just to the poor in spirit, but to
the have-nots and
the nobodies and
the hungry and
the homeless and
the forgotten and
the broken and
the discarded.

Jesus says that he has come to bring them the good news
that things are about to get better for them, that God's
favor will be upon them, that they will inherit the earth.

To proclaim release to the captives, he says.
Not just release to those who are imprisoned spiritually
by some personal struggle, but to people who are locked
away in real prison cells

for resisting and protesting and plotting against the brutality of the Roman military occupation.

To proclaim recovery of sight to the blind, he says.
This is not the *Amazing Grace* kind of
I-once-was-blind-but-now-I-see blind people.
Jesus is going to restore sight to those
who physically cannot see,
who everyday go unseen,
those with all kinds of physical disabilities
and conditions and diseases that have
somehow marked them as
different,
broken,
untouchable,
unworthy.

To set at liberty those who are oppressed, he says.
Jesus is going to liberate those who have been
crushed or held down by systems of
injustice and oppression,
simply because of their race,
their religion,
their nationality,
their Jewishness,
their zip codes.

To proclaim the acceptable year of the Lord, he says.

Jesus is going to announce the arrival of the Jubilee Year in which, every 50 years, according to Hebrew law, all debts must be cancelled, so that people are not crippled by a lifetime of debt, and indentured servants must be set free, so that nobody is ever sentenced to a lifetime of slavery, and ancestral lands taken by lenders as collateral are to be returned to their original owners, so that no one is ever condemned to a lifetime of generational homelessness.

All this profoundly human, social, down-to-earth,
real-world work in the ordinary world is how Jesus
understood the divine project of *salvation*.

Do you see how different it is from what we've been
told about salvation?

THE PITCH

When I was in college, a guy from down the hall knocked
on my dorm room door and
showed me a hand-drawn picture of a great chasm
and told me that
on one side of the chasm was humanity and
on the other side was God and
what separates us from God is sin and
sin is disobedience to the will of God but
the cross of Jesus is the bridge to God
and would I like to walk across that bridge right now?

And I said I knew last night's party got pretty crazy,
but is there something I'm not remembering?

What his hand-drawn picture and sales pitch
seemed to suggest was that baked into the universe
was this separation of
the human from the divine,
the unholy from the holy,
earthly things from heavenly things,
physical things from spiritual things.

God, according to his logic, is too holy for this messy
world. We must abandon the mess to get to God.

But Jesus had a very different view of sin and salvation.
Jesus came to redeem the mess. Jesus came to save his
people from themselves.

When Jesus preached his first sermon, his people were living under Roman military occupation. Visit Palestine today and you'll see that the tables have been turned—the ones who were once occupied are now occupiers—but the awfulness and ugliness of occupation, the despair and seething anger, the hopelessness and trauma of living under the heel of the oppressor always looks the same, and always leads to the same tragic outcomes—
violence,
bloodshed,
war,
tear gas,
tanks,
terror,
intimidation, and
death.

The Jews of Jesus' day were tired of emperors who kept them in poverty, laws that kept them in prisons, slavery that kept them in chains, and soldiers and taxes and tanks and decrees that kept them under submission.

For Jesus, sin was far more than personal disobedience. Sin was the system that kept people in poverty, slavery, fear, and misery—the inevitable outcomes of missing the mark, the *culpable disturbance of shalom*.

In his first sermon, Jesus asks—
How can we be *saved* if there are whole parts of our lives, our relationships, our communities, our world, that are impoverished and diminished?

How can we be saved when we are surrounded by un-peace?

The word *salvation* comes from the Latin, *salvus*. It means well-being, wholeness. It implies there is no salvation apart from the whole. Just as our bodies can't be healthy or whole if our spirits are unwell, neither can our society be healthy or whole if some of the people within it are unwell, or hungry, or hurting, or oppressed.

Salvation is never purely personal. The way Jesus understood it, people are not saved until the whole universe is restored to wholeness.

INSTRUCTIONS FOR
HOW TO SAVE OURSELVES

Jesus offered his people some clear tactics for how to achieve this wholeness in first-century Palestine.

> Love your enemies and pray for those who persecute you.[5]
> If anyone strikes you on the right cheek, turn the other also.
> If anyone forces you to go one mile, go also the second mile.[6]

This is how we save ourselves from ourselves and save the whole world.

Perhaps these enemy-loving,
cheek-turning,
second-mile-going tactics sound to you
like Jesus is saying
grit your teeth and bear it,
take your lumps,
accept your fate,
don't fight back,
just walk away.

But the late New Testament scholar Walter Wink famously argued that this was all about how to reclaim your humanity and dignity in the face of dehumanizing systems and humiliating actions.

If someone strikes you on one cheek,
you offer them your other cheek as a way of saying,
I'm still on my feet,
I'm still here,
you tried to shame me,
but I'm a human being, just like you.

If a Roman soldier forces you to carry his backpack
for one mile,
you carry it a second mile as a way of saying,
I'm not a victim,
I'm not your tool,
I'm not powerless,
I'm still standing.[7]

Jesus believed we could save ourselves and the whole
world not by abandoning our humanity but by embracing
it, not by sacrificing our dignity but by reclaiming it, not
by defeating the enemy but by transforming him, not
by grasping for power but by establishing *shalom*—the
bringing together of opposites:

Jews and Gentiles,
the powerful and the powerless,
Pharisees and centurions,
the mighty and the lowly,
the free and the slave,
and lots and lots of enemies.

It turned out to be a radical idea that achieved limited
success. The people of Jesus' day mostly rejected his
vision of salvation. In the end, the Messiah was crucified
by the oppressor who wielded the power and the
oppressed who pursued it as their only viable alternative.

Millions since have come to know of Jesus, and some
have come to believe in him, but few have come to trust
in his implausible vision of *shalom*—this radical, divinely

hatched notion that love can bring opposites together and turn enemies into friends.

Those who *have* embraced some form of this vision are enduring witnesses to its impact in the modern world, reminding us that the universe bends toward *shalom* for those who dare to work for it. Such witnesses include:

Mahatma Gandhi,
Dorothy Day,
Martin Luther King Jr.,
Leymah Gbowee,
Emily Greene Balch,
Mairead Maguire,
Gene Sharp,
Bob Marley,
Nelson Mandela.

AN ENLARGED HEART

What does it mean to be saved?

It's more than a transactional event that takes away our sins. It's a relational experience that, over time, leads to a kind of spaciousness of spirit within us.

Theologian Bernard Loomer
described this spaciousness as
an enlarged heart,
the stature of our soul,
the range and depth of our love,
our capacity for relationships,
the volume of life we can take into our being and
still maintain our integrity and individuality,
the intensity and variety of outlook we can entertain
without feeling defensive or insecure,
the strength of our spirit to encourage others to be
uniquely themselves.[8]

It's almost always risky. It's at times messy and complicated. It's a lifelong undertaking. It never ends.

Did you know that lobsters never stop growing? The largest lobster on record is about fifty years old and weighs in at forty-five pounds. But lobsters of this size and age are rare because it's risky to mature as a lobster.

Every few months a lobster sheds its exoskeleton. Releasing its shell is an exhausting process that leaves the flesh exposed and vulnerable. To grow, it must regularly let go of that spiny, tough exterior that makes it look so intimidating. Failure to rid itself of its outer shell would mean death by the very structure it previously created.

When a lobster's inner being has outgrown its shell, the shedding process ensues.

The lobster swallows large amounts of water, causing it to swell. Eventually, the internal pressure begins to separate the *carapace*, which is the part of its shell that protects its head and body.

Next, the lobster pops its eyes out of their holes, rendering itself temporarily blind.

Then begins the slow struggle of wrenching the flesh of its large pincer claws through its much smaller joints.

After the claw-flesh is free, the lobster is finally liberated from its shell with a flip of its tail.

But once free, the lobster flops around—exhausted, helpless, and vulnerable—as it waits for its new shell to harden.

If you've ever seen the cooked meat of a lobster, you've likely observed the pinkish color on its outer edge. This pink flesh is its emerging shell. The lobster's new outer structure is birthed out of what was there before.

The lobster is a metaphor for what's called *adaptive presence*. It knows what we all know—
we live and grow by daring to break free
from all that confines us.

BORN AGAIN AND AGAIN AND AGAIN

Maybe this is what Jesus meant when he told a man named Nicodemus one night that *no one can see the kingdom of God without being born from above.*[9]

Have you ever heard the sound of a baby's first cry?
It sounds like "Owh" because childbirth is painful not only for the mother but for the one being born.

So it is for those who, as Jesus says,
are born from above.

Perhaps we can think of salvation in terms of three births, each of which coincides with three necessary deaths.

The first birth comes when we discover that God loves and accepts us personally, unconditionally, impartially. When God's grace is implanted in our hearts, the work of enlarging our hearts begins.

Just days before Jesus preached his first sermon, he heard the voice of God at his baptism saying, "You are my Son, the Beloved; with you I am well pleased."[10]

This is the moment of our first birth, when we discover that we are God's beloved, that God takes delight in us.

This first birth coincides with the death of the illusion that we are somehow unlovable or unworthy of God's love, or that we do not need it. Here, we die to our guilt, our shame, the power of the false self, our pride, and our self-centeredness.

You can see this first birth in the story about a man named Zacchaeus—a chief tax collector and resident schmuck who was despised by the people he exploited. Jesus came to his home. They shared a meal. They talked. Zacchaeus experienced grace in that encounter. He felt God's acceptance and chose to hang up his tax collector's credential for good.

And Jesus said to Zacchaeus, "Today, salvation has come to this house."[11]

It's a beautiful story. But some Christians stop there on their own journey—never journeying beyond their first birth. They say, *I'm loved. I'm saved. I'm on the Jesus Team.* And their souls stop enlarging and expanding.

Which is why a second birth is necessary—one which leads to the discovery that God loves everyone—even the last and the least,
the enemy and the adversary,
your crazy uncle from Enid and
the people you find exceedingly difficult to love.

God loves everyone. This can be hard to accept.

It requires us to die to the illusion that God hates all the same people we do, that in God's calculus there must be winners and losers because even God's love has its limits.

This second birth can be painful. It can be hard to accept that we're special-not-so-special. The story of the prophet Jonah reminds us that God loves even Ninevites and shows mercy to all who experience a change of heart.

When we experience this second birth in our lives, it changes how we treat others. We find ourselves willing to forgive them when they hurt us. We give people second chances. We might even pray for our enemies and feed them and eat with them. We lead with curiosity about their stories rather than judgment.

Some Christians never experience this second birth. But if they do, they have a real chance at experiencing a third birth, which happens when we reorient our whole lives around the radical teachings of Jesus about the true nature of salvation and how God intends to save the world.

This new orientation calls us not only to *accept* others but to *actively work to liberate them*—from destructive behaviors like addiction or materialism or greed or vengeance,
from destructive social systems of injustice, oppression, bigotry, poverty,
and from the vicious cycle of violence, bloodshed, and death from which Jesus came to save his people.

This third birth opens us to a way of living in this world that sees the other—even the enemy—as worthy of laying down our lives for. And it requires us to die to the popular illusion that our Christian faith shouldn't ever be political or prophetic because being a Christian and going to church is all about being a good person and practicing kindness and keeping everything spiritual.

Like the lobster, this daring process of birth and death and rebirth happens over and over for us throughout our lives. Our hearts never stop enlarging as long as we lean into grace with courage and curiosity.

YOU'VE GOT TO LOVE 'EM ALL

Are you saved?

Jesus never asked that question.

Maybe the better question is,
How enlarged is your soul?

I read about the late preacher and civil right activist Will Campbell, who, in 1957, was one of four people who escorted the nine black students who integrated Little Rock's Central High School. When the hate mail from racists poured in, Campbell struggled with the uneasy feeling that he hated those bigots as much as they hated him. He had to die to the belief that God hated all the same people he hated. He realized that he'd become little more than a "doctrinaire social activist" instead of a follower of Jesus.

He wrote about the difficult journey of reorienting his life around God's love for all people. He came to understand the nature of tragedy, and concluded that one who understands the nature of tragedy can never take sides.

He experienced that third birth. He started sipping whiskey with the Ku Klux Klan. He officiated their funerals and weddings. He befriended the Grand Dragon of North Carolina, Bob Jones. He visited Klan members when they were sick. He became known as the "Chaplain to the Klan."

But he slowly won them over.

Then, something unexpected happened: the hate mail started coming in from liberals.

But his answer, which he repeated countless times over his life, was always the same:
"If you're gonna love one, you've got to love 'em all."[12]

This is how you can save yourself and the whole world.

Enlarged hearts.
Spacious souls.
Being born over and
over and
over again.

Chapter 8

"poof"

the end, with god

February 17, 1600.

That was the date when the Italian scientist and philosopher Giordano Bruno was convicted of heresy by the Roman Inquisition and sentenced to death after a seven-year trial. Peering through his telescope, Bruno had become convinced that Copernicus before him was right: the earth really did rotate around the sun—not the other way around, as the Bible suggests. Earth was not the center of the universe—the apple of God's eye—after all. In fact, the universe, said Bruno, wasn't even alone. Earth was just one planet among an infinite number of planets, in one of an infinite number of galaxies—a *plurality of worlds*, as he called it.

The church suddenly had a public relations crisis on its hands. Bruno's teachings might be true, they said, but they couldn't be reconciled with the Bible and church doctrine.

WE DON'T TALK ABOUT BRUNO

The Bruno affair was the O.J. Simpson trial of the Early Modern Era—only in Bruno's case, the glove fit. Bruno refused to renounce what he knew was scientifically true. At his trial, he also added a few choice words about his views on the doctrine of the Virgin Mary, which, it turned out, did not help his defense.

When Bruno was convicted of heresy and sentenced to death, he told his judges, "Perhaps your fear in passing judgment on me is greater than mine in receiving it."

That didn't seem to help his case either. He was handed over to his executioners, with his tongue in a gag, taken from the courtroom to the Campo de' Fiori where he was hung upside down naked and burned alive at the stake.

Thirty-three years later, in Rome, the astronomer and physicist, Galileo Galilei, also stood trial before the Inquisition. For Galileo, the heliocentric universe was a truth that could no longer be denied or silenced. It was irrefutable. But facing charges of heresy and possible death, Galileo ultimately recanted his teachings. Knowing how badly it went for Bruno, who could blame him?

Under oath, Galileo denied that the earth moves around the sun, even as, according to legend, he muttered under his breath, "And yet it moves!"

He was found guilty of heresy and sentenced to house arrest, where he spent the remainder of his remarkable life.

TUG OF WAR

The history of the universe is a story about a massive tug-of-war—

not just between scientists like Bruno or Galileo
and the church,
but between the expansion of the big bang,
which drove the matter of the world apart
13.7 billion years ago,
and the relentless pull of gravity,
which has been trying to make all that matter
come back together ever since.

At some future point in time, we know that
either expansion or gravity will finally win this
epic tug-of-war contest.

That the universe will eventually die is, sadly, a certainty.
How it will die, nobody really knows for sure.

If the forces of expansion triumph, the galaxies will
continue to recede from one another, black holes will
eventually dominate the universe, and temperatures
will approach absolute zero—minus 459.67 degrees
on the Fahrenheit scale. Scientists fittingly call this
theory the *big chill*.

If, on the other hand, the forces of gravity prevail, the
present expansion will be halted and reversed. All matter
in the universe will eventually fall back into a cosmic
melting pot. The universe that began with the *big bang* will
end, according to this theory, in the *big crunch*.[1]

Don't lose too much sleep over this. This cosmic tug of
war will take tens of billions of years before a winner is
declared.

But don't either of these rather bleak scenarios challenge
the ancient belief that
we are here for a reason,
that the universe is going somewhere
and becoming something,
that there's some divine intention or aim for all of this,

that God is calling all creation to beauty, *shalom*, enjoyment, and adventure?

Maybe it's better to reframe the question, because how we conceive of the death of the universe is not fundamentally any different than how we conceive of our own individual deaths. The questions are the same—

How must we live today? And, Is there a presence to be trusted for a future beyond this mortal life?

Humans have been asking these questions for millennia—long before we had any notion of what a planet even was, let alone that Earth is one of eight planets in our solar system circling the sun at about 60,000 miles an hour while rotating at the equator at 1,000 miles an hour in a solar system that's moving at over 550,000 miles an hour in a universe that's tens of millions of miles wide.

Do you ever feel like you're going a million miles an hour?

"Life moves pretty fast," said the Gen X prophet Ferris Bueller. "If you don't stop and look around once in a while, you could miss it."[2]

WHAT IF?

Here we are—all eight billion of us—hurtling through space on the back of what amounts to a grain of sand in an infinitely expanding universe, more and more conscious of the fact that whatever will happen to Earth will ultimately happen to us, that our destiny, for better or worse, is tied to that of Earth.

In 2003 NASA astronomers from the Jet Propulsion Laboratory's Sentry Earth impact monitoring system

peered through their telescopes and gave us a date:
March 21, 2014.[3]

Then they gave us a name: QQ47. That's what they called
a 4-billion-year-old asteroid they were tracking that is
three-quarters of a mile in diameter,
weighing two billion tons,
tearing through space at 22 miles per second
in our general direction.

Based on their observations, QQ47 had a 1 in 250,000
chance of impacting Earth on March 21, 2014.

This would have been our extinction event.

A lot of people said, 1 in 250,000?
Those are impossible odds. *It'll never happen.*

And yet those same people will buy lottery tickets
with a 1 in 300 million chance of winning because,
as they say, *it just might happen.*

March 21, 2014, came and went and QQ47 turned out to
be nothing to worry about after all.

But what if the odds had been higher?
Would it have changed how we live?

THE END OF THE WORLD
AS WE KNOW IT

For centuries, Christians have been obsessed with the end
of the world. End times speculation was popularized in
recent years by the fictional *Left Behind* novels, in which
the faithful are raptured to heaven while nonbelievers are
left behind to suffer through the cosmic extinction event
known as the Great Tribulation.

According to this view, you'll know the end times have

arrived when the world undergoes
political and economic crises,
global pandemics,
environmental catastrophe,
military conflicts—
all the disasters that, come to think of it,
are pretty much happening right now.

Some people love to talk about the end times.
It's a convenient framework that explains why
the world is in such bad shape
and why it's not necessary to do anything about it.

Climate change? COVID-19? Military conflicts around the world? Palestine?

Some Christians argue that not only should we *not* worry about such things, but we should welcome them as clear signs that the end is near.

It's *cringe-and-fringe* Christianity. It's popular and profitable. But it's unbiblical.

Why do a growing number of people struggle to believe in God—or at least the God they've been told about, who seems so irrelevant and *fantasy-landy*?

Maybe it's because too many Christians today are so obsessed with the *second coming* of Christ that they've neglected to follow the Christ who came the first time.

Where does all this apocalyptic thinking come from?

NOTES FROM THE UNDERGROUND

Much of Scripture, particularly the letters to the early Christian churches throughout first century Asia Minor, were written with a profound sense of the apocalyptic.

For early Christians, apocalyptic thinking was sparked by the violent, relentless persecution at the hands of a succession of Roman emperors who each demanded that they be worshiped as the *son of God*. Refusing to worship the emperor as *Lord* became a state crime punishable by death.

It's impossible to imagine the terrors and horrors the early church endured—all these tiny, vulnerable communities of Christians, designated as enemies of the state, traitors deserving of death. Families were torn apart, friends and loved ones were betrayed, outed, arrested, executed.

Living through such persecution, the early Christians wondered where history was headed. Is there some ultimate meaning to all this suffering?

Apocalyptic literature sought to answer this question.

The book of Revelation is perhaps the most elaborate, enigmatic, and most misunderstood work of apocalyptic literature ever conceived. Written by a pastor to a local church during this time of persecution, Revelation speaks about the powers and principalities of his context with raw symbolism and imagery of
dragons,
plagues,
whores,
horses,
beasts with swords protruding from their mouths,
lakes of fire.

Rome, the evil persecutor, is called Babylon.

Why all the metaphors?

Because the book of Revelation was written as subversive protest literature. It was cryptic, underground communication written to give Christians hope that Rome would get what it deserved and the faithful would be redeemed. Rome would fall, and a new city, a new creation, the New Jerusalem, would rise. It would be a garden, like the garden in the creation poem in the book of Genesis, where there would be no more death or suffering.

The book of Revelation gave people genuine hope that God would not abandon the world but redeem it.

SEEKING A FRIEND FOR THE END OF THE WORLD

But while the book of Revelation continues to get a lot of attention today, there's an alternative vision of the end times in the Letter to the Ephesians. It speaks to these same fears and hopes that Christians had about the future. But whereas Revelation reads like a graphic sci-fi novel, Ephesians reads more like a sermon.

In the letter, the writer of Ephesians reaches back into ancient Scripture for an idea that would communicate truth. He goes all the way back to the exile, about five hundred years earlier, to the book of Jeremiah, who had written words of encouragement to the exiles. Like the early Christians in Rome, the exiles in Babylon were praying for God to end their suffering, to defeat the forces of oppression in a final battle.

But, instead, the prophet Jeremiah wrote to the exiles in peaceful images:

> I have loved you with an everlasting love.
>
> I am going to . . . gather them from the farthest parts of the earth.
> With weeping they shall come, and with consolations I will lead them back.[4]

Jeremiah was prophesying that the history of God's people would not culminate in violence or death or the destruction of the world.
It's all heading toward restoration and reunion with God.
Creation will flourish,
food will be abundant,
the young will dance and the old will watch in delight,
mourning will be transformed into joy,
the people will weep tears of gladness.

This is the imagery we find in the Letter to the Ephesian Christians who were praying for Christ to return. The writer echoes Jeremiah's image of God "gathering up" all creation.

> With all wisdom and insight he has made known to us the mystery of his will, according to his good pleasure that he set forth in Christ, as a plan for the fullness of time, to gather up all things in him, things in heaven and things on earth.[5]

That's a radically different understanding of apocalypse—
a moment in time when God gathers all things
to God's self,
an experience of *shalom*,
the bringing together of all things,
even opposing, disparate things,
into oneness and wholeness with God.

This message is woven throughout the Bible. It says, I know it's difficult—the hardship, the injustice, the suffering, the pain you're enduring. But don't give up. Keep working for what is right and good in the world. Don't concede or grow cynical. It's all headed somewhere: *shalom*.

You won't find that message in the *Left Behind* books. But it's everywhere in the Bible. God does not plan to abandon this world, but to gather up all things, restore all things, unite all things in *shalom*—right here, in this world.

Jesus preached this vision relentlessly and practiced it endlessly. He was the embodiment of that *fullness of time* in which the lost are found, the outcasts restored to community, the sick healed, the hungry fed, the sinner forgiven, the enemy befriended, the dead raised to life.

Shalom.
Wholeness.
Unity in God.

Jesus, the prophets, the ancient teachers all said the same thing: history is ultimately headed toward *shalom*.

What about you?

WHAT ARE YOU LIVING FOR?

There's a theological word for how we talk about our hopes and fears of the future: eschatology. It's from the Greek *eschatos*, meaning *last*, and *logos*, meaning the *study of*.

Eschatology is the study of last things—how all of this is going to end.

Why is eschatology so important?

Because how we think this is all going to end determines how we live in the here and now.

Eschatology shapes our behaviors and attitudes.
Last things tell us what to do about present things.
What we hope for influences what we live and work for.

My wife, Lori, works as a behavior interventionist with special needs children who've been diagnosed with spectrum disorders—most notably, autism. Because many of her students are nonverbal, her work involves teaching them to how to communicate and express themselves in nonverbal ways. To incentivize and reinforce communication and other desired behaviors, she uses a reward system with a variety of reinforcements. Sometimes all it takes is a single Tic Tac, or a Barbie to play with, or free time on a computer. What makes her so extraordinarily effective at her job is her uncanny, almost Yoda-like ability to quickly decipher what specific reinforcement will induce the desired behavior in her students.

One of her most inspiring stories was about a particular student who would have daily, lengthy, often self-injurious meltdowns. She'd retreat into her own world, bang her head against the floor, and refuse to engage for long stretches of her day. Lori struggled to make that all-important connection that would bring this girl back to the real world.

Until one afternoon, when she overheard this little girl humming a song in the bathroom, unaware that Lori could hear her. She was completely nonverbal, but she hummed the song almost perfectly. Lori immediately recognized the tune as Kelly Clarkson's "Stronger (What Doesn't Kill You)". She immediately removed her iPhone from her backpack and downloaded the song.

Later that same day, when the girl had yet another major, violent meltdown and refused to engage, Lori took out her phone, pressed the play button on the music app, and—almost as if on cue—the little girl immediately jumped to her feet and began dancing and spinning and bouncing and twirling with her arms in the air.

Later that evening, Lori downloaded every Kelly Clarkson song on iTunes, and every day thereafter, whenever she needed to engage and incentivize this girl, she finally had the key. Lori said it was the most breathtaking part of her day—that moment when she'd hit the play button and watch this beautiful girl suddenly come to life and shimmy like Shakira.

What we hope for shapes what we live and work for. And, for most of us, there are at least two ways to live hopefully in this world.

One way is to hope passively for that *fullness of time* to arrive,
putting our faith in the rapture,
believing that because God has an eternal evacuation plan for the faithful,
we can let the earth go to pieces.

But the more faithful way to live is to choose daily, like Jesus, to embody that *fullness of time* in everything we do, trusting the promises of Ephesians—
that God will not abandon creation,
that nothing is too broken to be redeemed,
that the very things we want to escape from or write off are the same things that God, in love,
wants to gather unto God's self and reclaim in the *fullness of time.*
To live every day believing that no one—indeed, nothing in all creation—will be left behind.

How do we do this?

THIS IS YOUR LIFE

Kieran Setiya, a professor of philosophy at MIT, says the Greeks believed there were two kinds of activities in our lives. They called them "telic" and "atelic" activities.[6]

Telic activities—from the Greek *telos*, meaning *purpose*— are goals with endpoints. A telic activity is something that can be finished, like mowing the lawn, reading this book, or bathing your cat. With telic activities, once you reach the goal, you're finished.

But where we find meaning is by attending to atelic activities. Atelic activities are ongoing endeavors that have no definitive endpoint, such as hanging out with friends, practicing prayer or meditation or yoga, playing a game of catch with your child, or feeding the hungry at the local shelter. There's no end to atelic activities. You can't say, "I just fed 120 hungry people today and solved world hunger."

How much of your life is consumed by telic activities?
Do you find yourself
marching through your day trying to check off
one more task,
respond to one more email,
complete one more project,
cross off one more chore from the list?

Telic activities *do* make the world go around.
If we didn't do them,
we wouldn't get anywhere.

But they're also so alluring.

We love to check boxes.
We love that sense of completion.
But what makes our lives complete?

I've officiated countless funerals over the years. But never once have I officiated a funeral in which somebody took the microphone and said,
"Jim was a great man. I mean, *wow*, he mowed his lawn dutifully every week—*what a legacy*."

Or "Mary was super responsive with her emails—I'll just never forget that about her."

Some things in life you can't check off a list.

When we ask,
What will God do with planet Earth at the end of time?
what we're really asking is,
What will we do on planet Earth in the time that we have
on the Earth?

Because what will happen to us
at the end of our time on Earth
is what will happen to Earth at the end of time.

God will gather all things unto God's self.
Nothing will be lost.
All that has ever been will be forever preserved by God.

Alfred North Whitehead said it best,

> The image—and it is but an image—the image under
> which this operative growth of God's nature is best
> conceived, is that of a tender care that nothing be lost.
> . . . The consequent nature of God is his judgment on
> the world. He saves the world as it passes into the
> immediacy of his own life. It is the judgment of a ten-
> derness which loses nothing that can be saved. It is
> also the judgment of a wisdom which uses what in
> the temporal world is mere wreckage.[7]

As it says in the book of Revelation, "See, I am making all
things new. . . . It is done! I am the Alpha and the Omega,
the Beginning and the End."[8]

WHAT HAPPENS WHEN WE DIE?

When I was pastoring a church in San Diego, a local
reporter would drop by a different church each Sunday
morning. He'd sit through the service and then pull the
pastor aside afterward to ask for a response to his only
question—

"What happens when we die?"

He would then feature the pastor's response in his newspaper column the following week.

It was a wildly popular column for reasons
I cannot explain, because every pastor seemed to have an answer that sounded a lot like every other pastor's answer. None were very biblically grounded, but they always zeroed in on
God's judgment,
heaven and hell,
sin and salvation.

Preachy stuff. Creepy stuff. The kind of stuff that often leads people to choose life after God.

Some people are so certain and descriptive about what happens after we die,
despite having never made the journey themselves.

Some people seem so certain and confident about where *they* will go after they die,
despite what everyone else happens to think of them.

That reporter never showed up at my church to ask me his question. But if he had, I would've pointed him to a story from Luke, about an influential man who one day asks Jesus, "What must I do to inherit eternal life?"[9]

Isn't that the real question?

Not just, "What happens when we die?"
But "What will happen to *me* after I die?"
As in, "Is there life *for me* after death?"
As in, "What must *I* do to get eternal life?"

A lot of Christians usually come back
with answers like—
confess your sins,
pray the sinner's prayer,

give your life to Jesus,
and believe.

These are just some of the answers
you may have been told.
And these can be life-changing, life-giving
for many people.

I'm a big fan of confessing sins.
I pray daily.
I believe in God.
So, does that mean I'm in?

When this man comes to Jesus and asks him,
"What must I do to inherit eternal life?"
these aren't the answers Jesus gives him.

The answer Jesus gives to the man who wants to know
how to inherit eternal life is really strange:

Be faithful in marriage.
Do not murder.
Do not steal.
Do not tell lies about others.
Respect your father and mother.

You've probably heard of the Ten Commandments.
These are five of those ten.

But are you as confused as I am?
This is how we inherit eternal life?

That's weird. And what's even more weird is that
Jesus only names five of those Ten Commandments—
and the five Jesus names are not even remotely
religious or spiritual.

Of the Ten Commandments, the first four commandments
are what we'd characterize as spiritual—

Do not worship any god except me.

Do not make idols.
Do not misuse my name.
Remember the Sabbath Day.

These four commandments are all about
our relationship with God.

But Jesus doesn't include these commandments
in his response to the man's question,
"What must I do to inherit eternal life?"

The remaining six commandments
are all about our human relationships.
In his answer, Jesus mentions five of them.
He leaves out the tenth commandment about *coveting*.

We don't know why he left this one out.
Maybe Jesus was jonesing on the rich guy's sandals.

He only lists these five commandments:

Be faithful in marriage.
Do not murder.
Do not steal.
Do not tell lies about others.
Respect your father and mother.

They're all about our human relationships.

Does this story make any sense to you?

What starts out as a question about *eternal life*
turns into a conversation on five commandments
about how to live in this *earthly life*.

The entire story hinges on this one phrase, *eternal life*.
What is it?

It's not what we've been told it is. At least, not exactly.

TIMES LIKE THESE

We often equate *eternal life* with going to heaven
when we die.

But this isn't what Jesus believed or taught.
It's not what the ancient Hebrews believed or taught.

Jesus never taught about how to *get into heaven*.
He taught about how to inherit *eternal life*.

To understand the difference, it helps to distinguish
between space and time. Jesus didn't understand eternal
life primarily in spatial terms, as we moderns typically do.

Jesus talked about eternal life in temporal terms.

Like all Jews of his day, Jesus understood time in terms
of *ages*—or *eons*. *Eon*, from the Greek, *aion*, is the root
word of *eternal*, from the Greek, *aionion*.

Jesus saw the temporal world as composed of two ages:
this age and what he often called *the age to come*. The
age to come was not an age beyond or outside of earthly
time and space. It was just an age after the age we
happen to be in right now.

Jesus perceived the world not spatially—as in,
there's an earth down here and a heaven up there—
but in terms of present and future—as in,
there's this world and another world that is coming.

This was how the Old Testament prophets saw the world.
This age and the age to come.
They all believed the universe was headed toward some
ultimate purpose or aim.
That purpose would be fulfilled
in the age to come,
which would happen
in this world.

The prophets described the fulfillment of that purpose as
a time of *shalom* in which justice and peace would prevail,
a time in which there would be no war,
no weeping,
no sickness,
no hunger,
no crime,
no racism,
no refugees,
no suffering.

And no social media,
no cable news,
no angry or snarky tweets,
no email.

The prophets called it *shalom*—an age in which all things
would be gathered into oneness and wholeness with God.

In the age to come,
God would pour out God's spirit on all flesh, and our sons
and daughters would prophesy, and our elders would
dream dreams, and our young would see visions.[10]

In the age to come,
truth would be in our mouths and no wrong
would be found on our lips,[11]
the lame and exhausted would mount up
with wings like eagles,
run and not be weary, walk and not faint,[12] and
all people would be given new wine, new crops,
new grain, new hearts.[13]

The age to come would bring
renewal,
redemption,
restoration,
wholeness,
shalom.

It would happen not in some other world, but in this world.

Some Christians believe that God is so disappointed with this world that, as a last resort, God will create a whole new one—a heavenly world—that only some are worthy to enter. But the God of the Bible loves this world too much to abandon it and intends to redeem it rather than devise some divine evacuation plan to bail us out of it.

This God comes to us,
comes to this world,
to this time and
woos us,
calls us
to live out that prayer,
"Thy kingdom come, thy will be done,
on earth as it is in heaven."

This kingdom, this *age to come*,
is the world we are all called to co-create with God.

And Jesus tells the man how to do that—how we can all experience the age to come in the here and now. He didn't give us an exhaustive list. He just started with the basics:

Be faithful in marriage.
Do not murder.
Do not steal.
Do not tell lies about others.
Respect your father and mother.

Profoundly relational advice.

Live this way, says Jesus, and the age to come will come.

This is not higher-level coursework. These simple commandments constitute the most basic foundation of human community. We will never experience *the age to come* if we cannot master the ABCs of this age:
integrity,
kindness,

compassion,
mutuality,
honor,
truthfulness.

All the prophets, Jesus, the ancient rabbis taught that
we are partners in creating eternal life,
co-creators with God of the age to come.

And it starts by living the commandments of God.
It's how we bring the age to come into the here and now.
Heaven on earth.
Shalom.
Eternal life.

JUST LIKE HEAVEN

But still, you ask—what happens when we die?
Is there a heaven, too?

The ancient Hebrews, Jesus, Paul—they also spoke
of a realm, a place, a dimension of God's creation that
transcends this world, where all is as God intends it to be.

It's a realm where that age to come is already happening.
On earth as is it is in heaven, we pray, because that
shalom of God *is* happening. It's not just an aim. It's a
present reality. Somewhere—in some dimension of space
we cannot see or touch, in some dimension of time we
cannot measure.

But not even Jesus told us exactly what it looks like,
how it works,
where it is,
or what form it takes.

Jesus spoke of heaven and the afterlife almost exclusively
in parables and allegories. He told stories that conceived

of heaven not as a *place*, but as an *experience*. He often likened that experience to attending a wedding feast, or a party, or a banquet. There are fifteen allusions in the Gospels in which Jesus speaks of eternal life as a party-like experience, most of which suggest that God's invitation list is long and not nearly as exclusive as we might expect.[14] Everyone is invited to God's party. Anyone can attend God's banquet—both the good *and* the not-so-good.[15] Only many will choose not to attend for various reasons: some have work to finish or businesses to run; others have already committed to attending someone else's party; still others have scheduling conflicts or an assortment of other very excellent excuses;[16] and a small handful are sadly just too burned out, like lamps that have simply run out of oil.[17]

God seems to have a hard time giving away *heaven*. Maybe that's because we prefer God to be just a little more selective and exclusive. We don't want to sit at the banquet table with just *anyone*, and especially not *everyone*. God, heaven, eternal life isn't supposed to work that way.

According to our human logic,
there are good places and bad places
for good people and bad people,
and most of us are more than happy
to suggest to God how, in the end,
the Big Sort should play out.

Good people prefer a judge and courtroom where the Big Sort can ultimately take place. But how many times did Jesus refer to eternal life or heaven as a courtroom scene?

Once.

In the parable of the Last Judgment,[18] as it's often called.

In that story, some assumed they'd been doing all the right things all their lives—which presumably made them *good people*. But as it turned out, they never got around to doing the most basic things in this world, which turned out to be ultimate things in the eyes of God: feeding the hungry, visiting the prisoner, clothing the naked, caring for the sick.

Others did all these basic things without even knowing that they were ultimate things. They simply believed that, by doing them, they'd bring the *age to come* into *this age—shalom*, eternal life, in the here and now. They never presumed that anyone was watching, but they did these things anyway. They weren't driven by the fear of punishment or the hope of reward. They were driven purely by love. They were wooed, lured, called by the vision of *shalom* in the age to come.

No one had any idea that such basic things would all somehow be part of the final exam. And for those who failed to do them, the Big Sort didn't go down as planned. They didn't pass the test.

The parable suggests that we do not need to wait for the Big Sort. It reveals to us the urgency of waking up to the God who is already here—*in this age*—and often in disguise, calling and luring and persuading us to work for the *age to come* in the here and now.

Moment by moment. Day by day. Even unto death. Even after we die.

So, what happens when we die?

Whether, in this life,
we neglected or rejected the divine call,
missed the wedding banquet,
and failed the final exam,

or responded to the divine call,

feasted at the banquet table
and passed the final exam,

God,
even after our mortal life ceases,
never stops holding out possibilities for us
to respond to the divine call,
the everlasting woo,
to achieve that *good thought*, intention, aim,
that God has for us in the present moment.

We are forever in God's experience.
God is forever in our experience.
Nothing is ever lost.
All is preserved in and by and with God.
The experience never ends.
The experience will be different when our bodies die.
But it will never end.

We will always get to choose our next best step,
even after our bodily death.
We can always choose to ignore the lure, to reject the call.
Or we can choose to respond to it, to pursue it.
God's never-ending hope is that those who rejected
the divine call in this age might finally respond faithfully
to it in the age to come.
Some, however, might reject it forever.

But our hope in this age remains the hope in the age to
come, which is always that

> neither death, nor life, nor angels, nor rulers, nor
> things present, nor things to come, nor powers, nor
> height, nor depth, nor anything else in all creation will
> be able to separate us from the love of God.[19]

I don't know how a place called *hell* could ever fit into
this eternal hope we have and this endless, entangled,
inseverable love of God that Paul speaks of.

Even on my worst days, when I could probably name a few people I'd like to send there, I remind myself that nothing can separate them from the love of God. God will never stop calling them. And because the rest is pure speculation, we can at least live with this hope.

It's biblical,
it's rational,
it's purposeful, and
it's wonderfully promising.

What do you hope for?

In that unknowable realm of God's unending,
entangled, eternal love,
I hope I'll see my father,
and the friends and family members
who have gone before me,
and all the people I've loved and mourned and buried.

I hope I'll see those I misunderstood,
and those who misunderstood me in this realm.
Maybe we can understand someday what we couldn't
understand in the here and now.

I hope I'll see those who seemed to have rejected
God's call in this life—
all the people I might never have expected to see there
and all the people I wanted to write off
but God didn't.

And all the people who lived life after God
but all along were really living a life in pursuit of God.

I hope I'll see Gandhi there.
And the Buddha and Black Elk and the Dalai Lama.
And the seminary professor who pulled the gun on me.
And Morgan Freeman—because he's been in so many
movies about actually being there.

And dogs—because while there's a special place for cats, all dogs really should go to heaven.

But that's just me and my hope.

For all the doubting I've ever done, I always keep coming back to this ancient chorus the early Christians used to sing whenever they worshiped together. It went something like,

> As it was in the beginning
> is now and ever shall be,
> world without end.
> Amen.

They all seemed to know what so many of us are still trying to figure out:
Nothing is lost.
Not even the wreckage of this temporal world
in this present age.
All that ever has been,
all that now is,
all that shall be,
is forever preserved in God,
by God,
with God.

BOOK CLUB
DISCUSSION GUIDE

1. How would you describe "the God you no longer believe in"?
2. Do you find yourself challenged by questions of theodicy, or why an all-loving and all-powerful God does not stop bad things from happening? Do you consider this a problem that must be solved?
3. What is the difference between a God who works through relational power and one who works through unilateral power? Do you agree with the author's claim that God internalizes or feels what we feel in such a way that our experience influences God's experience?
4. If God's intention and aim for the whole world is *shalom*, what would that look like in your own life? Is it a far-off, ultimate hope, or something you could experience every day? What is our role in helping God bring about *shalom*?
5. Have you ever heard God spoken of as the Unmoved Mover or the Divine Watchmaker, powerful but unchanging? How do you describe what is changing about God and what is unchanging?

6. Does the idea of God being in everyone, and everyone and everything being part of God make God seem more awe-inspiring or less to you? Does it change the way you think of God?

7. Similarly, do you think science (or generally, knowing why certain things happen) makes God seem less mysterious or powerful? Is mystery inherent to God's wonder and glory?

8. What do Jesus' life and teachings tell you about the false duality between the physical and the spiritual? What is the effect on our faith if we persistently spiritualize the promises of physical healing Jesus talks about?

9. Does the image of a lobster continually outgrowing its exoskeleton, doing the hard and vulnerable work of removing the old shell and growing a new one, resonate with your spiritual journey? How so?

10. Is it hard for you to think about what might come after this life? How might the vision of "the age to come"—an age marked by *shalom* and everything God dreams for the world—change the way you think about God and life itself?

SPECIAL DISCOUNTS AVAILABLE

Most Westminster John Knox Press books are available at special quantity discounts when purchased in bulk by corporations, organizations, and special-interest groups.

For more information, please email SpecialSales@wjkbooks.com.

SMALL GROUP STUDY GUIDE

CHAPTER 1
"shh"   the problem of god

1. The author begins with the story of his professor's hypothetical question about God stopping a fired bullet. Do you find yourself challenged by questions of *theodicy*, or why an all-loving and all-powerful God does not stop bad things from happening? Do you consider this a problem that must be solved?

2. What do you think of Pascal's wager that it is safer or wiser to believe in God than to risk eternal punishment? Do you agree with Pascal that "reason impels you to believe"?

3. How might the opposite—"reason impedes your ability to believe"—be true instead?

4. Have you heard the "shhh" the author discusses— the implicit or explicit warning not to ask the hard questions about God? What questions seem most threatening to some people?

5. How would you describe "the God you no longer believe in"?

CHAPTER 2
"psst"   the call of god

1. If you imagine organized religion as your "boat in the storm," how do you decide when the challenge of hanging on is worth the risk of letting go?
2. Consider Walt Whitman's advice to "Re-examine all you have been told at school or church or in any book, dismiss whatever insults your own soul." What beliefs have you found to be insulting to your soul? How do you feel about the author's advice to, before discarding, "give them permission to exist, to sit beside you, to just be," and then, if you find they have no further value for you, "Tell them thanks for sharing, but it's time for them to move on now"?
3. In contrast to those things that insult your soul, what has "gladdened your soul and added beauty and wonder and joy to your life," as the author says?
4. Is there anywhere you see God currently at work in your life or in the world? Are there small or ordinary things presently beckoning or calling you toward greater meaning, beauty, or wonder?
5. What is the difference between a God who works through relational power and one who works through unilateral power? Can you identify with a call from God that sounds like "Psst. You could do this. You could be this"?

CHAPTER 3
"hmmm"   the aim of god

1. How do you feel about the idea that God has a plan for everything?
2. Have you ever looked to Jeremiah 29:11 as a promise for your own life? How does it change

your perspective to read "plans" as "intentions" or "thoughts"?

3. If God's intention and aim for the whole world is *shalom*, what would that look like in your own life? Is it a far-off, ultimate hope, or something you could experience every day? What is our role in helping God bring about *shalom*?

4. Do you agree with the Theodore Parker quote (often associated with Dr. Martin Luther King Jr.) that the moral arc of the universe "bends toward justice"? If so, do you see that as the work of God?

5. What do you think of the assertion that seeking *shalom* is not just about the future, or even the present, but also involves how we look at the past?

CHAPTER 4
"sheesh" the nature of god

1. Do you resonate with the phrase "a leap of doubt"? How might it compare to a "leap of faith"?

2. Have you ever heard God spoken of as the Unmoved Mover or the Divine Watchmaker? Have you ever thought of God as powerful but unchanging?

3. How do you describe what is changing about God and what is unchanging?

4. The author discusses the Hebrew terms for God, *Adonai* and *Elohim*, one used when describing God's intimate, earthy presence; and the other when speaking of God's mighty, cosmic power. Do you have different names for God when thinking of different attributes of God?

5. Do you agree with the author's claim that God internalizes or feels what we feel in such a way that our experience influences God's experience?

CHAPTER 5
"hum" the presence of god

1. When or where do you feel (or seek to feel) God's presence? Is it more often in or outside of the church or other traditionally religious places?
2. As the author asks in this chapter, have you ever had an experience in which you found yourself deeply aware of something beautiful or powerful? Have you ever sensed that there might be a presence humming behind the veil of reality, something unmistakably real but not altogether reasonable or explainable?
3. What significance do you see in the fact that the Hebrew and Greek words for spirit are the same words as for breath and wind?
4. Do you see theological significance in the concept of Caesar's Last Breath, or is it simply a scientific phenomenon? What does it mean to you?
5. Does the idea of God being in everyone, and everyone and everything being part of God make God seem more awe-inspiring or less to you? Does it change the way you think of God?

CHAPTER 6
"bzzz" the glory of god

1. What would you say gives life meaning?
2. Do you think science (or generally, knowing why certain things happen) makes God seem less mysterious? Is mystery inherent to God's wonder and glory?
3. The author suggests that Descartes's famous claim, "I think, therefore I am," has led to a modern worldview that values mind over matter and reason over belief. Do you see a distinction or conflict between human

reason and divine revelation? In your view, are faith and reason compatible?

4. The author quotes Alfred North Whitehead in saying that God is "an occasion, an event of subjective experience." Do you find this definition meaningful?

5. What is your response to the ancient Greek puzzle of Theseus's ship? Do you agree with how the author says Jesus would respond—that it's not about the planks at all? How might you apply this riddle to life today?

CHAPTER 7
"owh" the salvation of god

1. Have you ever been approached with the aggressive evangelism the author describes experiencing at a crusade event and in his college dorm? What was that experience like?

2. What do Jesus' life and teachings tell you about the false duality between the physical and the spiritual? What is the effect on our faith if we persistently spiritualize the promises of physical healing Jesus talks about?

3. The author says Jesus' vision for *shalom* had "limited success" in his lifetime. Do you agree? How successful would you say Jesus' vision has been over the past two thousand years?

4. Does the image of a lobster continually outgrowing its exoskeleton, doing the hard and vulnerable work of removing the old shell and growing a new one, resonate with your spiritual journey? How so?

5. Can you imagine reaching the "third birth" that the author describes, able to love one's enemy the way Will Campbell cared for the Klan members? How could you grow in that direction?

CHAPTER 8
"poof" the end, with god

1. What are your thoughts on how the world will end—fire, ice, expansion, contraction—or something else?
2. Why do you think Revelation's violent vision of the end times, in which persecutors get what's coming to them, is so much more popular with and well-known to modern Christians than prophetic imagery of God gathering all things together, lions laying down with lambs, etc.?
3. The author discusses *telic* and *atelic* activities. How does the way you spend your time break down across those categories? What are you doing that will last?
4. Why, when Jesus was asked about eternal life, did he talk about the things one does in this earthly life?
5. Is it hard for you to think about what might come after this life? How might the vision of "the age to come"—an age marked by *shalom* and everything God dreams for the world—change the way you think about God and life itself?

SPECIAL DISCOUNTS AVAILABLE

Most Westminster John Knox Press books are available at special quantity discounts when purchased in bulk by corporations, organizations, and special-interest groups.

For more information, please email SpecialSales@wjkbooks.com.

ACKNOWLEDGMENTS

Thank you to all the believers and doubters and skeptics and heretics at St. Andrew United Methodist Church whose theological imagination and endless curiosity created safe space for a sermon series that became this book.

To Lana Banbury, who can find a needle in any haystack and found more than a few while painstakingly reviewing countless drafts—at all hours of the day and night.

To all the professors and mentors and colleagues and parishioners and friends and even strangers who've ever dared to pull a loaded finger gun on me and ask some hard questions.

And to the growing community of *process* and *open and relational* thinkers committed to the urgent work of reconstructing the Christian faith for those who still see the beauty of God and can't say no.

NOTES

Chapter 1: "shh"   the problem of god

1. This famous treatise is laid out in *Pascal's Pensées*, now published widely in the public domain and found here: https://www .gutenberg.org/files/18269/18269-h/18269-h.htm.

2. C.S. Lewis, *The Problem of Pain* (1940; repr., London: HarperCollins Publishers, 2002), 105.

3. C.S. Lewis, *A Grief Observed* (1961; repr., London: HarperCollins Publishers, 2001), 29–30, 38.

4. Lewis, *Grief Observed*, 36.

5. Nicholas Wolterstorff, *Lament for a Son* (Grand Rapids: Eerdmans, 1987), 68.

6. Job 7:20.

7. https://plato.stanford.edu/entries/pascal/.

8. https://www.pewresearch.org/fact-tank/2017/09/06 /more-americans-now-say-theyre-spiritual-but-not-religious.

9. https://www.pewresearch.org/religion/2021/12/14/ about-three-in-ten-u-s-adults-are-now-religiously-unaffiliated.

10. Gen. 28:16.

Chapter 2: "psst"   the call of god

1. https://religionnews.com/2022/09/13/fewer-than-half-of -americans-may-be-christian-by-2070-according-to-new-projections/.

2. https://news.gallup.com/poll/393737/belief-god-dips-new-low.aspx.

3. Genesis 1.

4. This concept of God as "lure" originates from the groundbreaking thought and work of the early twentieth-century mathematician and philosopher, Alfred North Whitehead. Whitehead offered a new cosmology and metaphysics that challenged the conventional "substance-based" worldview of the day, offering instead a view of the world as "event-based" in which all creatures are "occasions" or "drops" of experience in the process of becoming. Nearly everything you'll read in this book has been influenced by Whitehead's process thought, which was later developed by theologians such as John B. Cobb, David Ray Griffin, Marjorie Hewitt Suchocki, Catherine Keller, Thomas Jay Oord, and Tripp Fuller (see his *Homebrewed Christianity* podcast) to name just a few. If you're interested in reading more about process theology or open and relational theology, just google these names, read their work, and be prepared to never see the world the same again.

5. I first came across these two conceptions of power in the work of the late philosopher and theologian, Bernard Loomer. I encourage you to read this essay, "Two Conceptions of Power," which you can find at https://www.religion-online.org/article/two-conceptions-of-power.

6. Alfred North Whitehead, *Process and Reality: An Essay in Cosmology*, rev. ed. (New York: Free Press, 1978), 342–43.

7. I first came across this breakthrough idea in John Cobb's book, *Jesus' Abba: The God Who Has Not Failed* (Minneapolis: Fortress Press, 2015), 3.

8. Matt. 6:9–13.

9. 1 Cor. 13:4–8a.

Chapter 3: "hmmm"   the call of god

1. Jer. 1:5.

2. Matt. 10:30.

3. Ps. 139:4.

4. Ps. 139:16.

5. Rom. 8:28.

6. Jer. 29:11.

7. This quote, later paraphrased by Martin Luther King Jr, is from a sermon preached by Theodore Parker, "Truth and the Intellect,"

in *Ten Sermons of Religion* (Boston: Crosby, Nichols, and Co.,1853). For the full text of the sermon, see https://archive.org/details /tensermonsofreli00inpark/page/38/mode/2up.

8. Isa. 11:6-9.

9. Kris Kristofferson, writer, composer and vocalist, "Help Me Make It Through the Night," track 5 on *Kristofferson*, Monument Records, 1970.

10. While I did not know John Claypool personally, his widow and my close friend, Ann Beard, tells me this line was one he used often in his sermons.

11. For more on this, see Søren Kierkegaard, "The Unhappiest One," in *Either/Or: A Fragment of Life* (New York: Penguin Random House, 1992) 209–222.

12. Exod. 3:1-6.

13. Rom. 7:14-24.

14. *The Office*, season 9, episodes 24 and 25, "Finale," written by Greg Daniels, directed by Ken Kwapis, aired May 16, 2013, on NBC.

Chapter 4: "sheesh"   the nature of god

1. Mal. 3:6.

2. Jas. 1:17.

3. Heb. 13:8.

4. Thomas O. Chisholm, "Great Is Thy Faithfulness."

5. Exod. 32:14.

6. Gen. 6:6.

7. Ps. 106:45a.

8. Jer. 18:8.

9. Amos 7:3a.

10. Gen. 18:22–33.

11. This is often referred to as dipolar or bipolar theism by process theologians, and was developed by, among others, the philosopher Charles Hartshorne.

12. God as "Poet of the World" is a concept introduced by Alfred North Whitehead, *Process and Reality: An Essay in Cosmology*, rev. ed. (New York: Free Press, 1978).

13. Gen. 2:7.

14. Gen. 2:4-7.

15. Lam. 3:22–23.

16. I'm inspired here by Thomas Jay Oord's illustration in his book *Open and Relational Theology: An Introduction to Life-Changing Ideas* (Grasmere, ID: SacraSage Press, 2021), 40–41.

17. John 11.

18. John 11:43.

Chapter 5: "hum"   the presence of god

1. Jane Fonda, "About My Faith," June 10, 2009, https://www.janefonda.com/2009/06/about-my-faith.

2. https://www.janefonda.com/2009/06/about-my-faith.

3. Frederick Buechner, *The Longing for Home: Recollections and Reflections* (San Francisco: HarperSanFrancisco, 1996), 126–27.

4. Gen. 1:2.

5. Ps. 139:7–10.

6. Job 27:3.

7. John 3:8.

8. Acts 17:25 (italics added).

9. See Plotinus, *The Enneads*.

10. Qur'an 15:28–29.

11. From Gandhi's 1931 speech at Kingsley Hall, London. You can view the entire video at https://www.ndtv.com/india-news/mahatma-gandhis-famous-speech-at-kingsley-hall-in-1931-565204.

12. Nikos Kazantzakis, *Report to Greco*, trans. P.A. Bien (New York: Simon and Schuster, 1965), 291.

13. John 17:21.

14. Rom. 8:26.

15. Hirokazu Kore-eda, dir., *After Life* (Japan: Engine Film, TV Man Union, 1998).

Chapter 6: "bzzz"   the glory of god

1. *Groundhog Day*, Danny Rubin, screenwriter (Culver City, CA: Columbia Pictures, 1993).

2. René Descartes. Discourse on the Method of Rightly Conducting One's Reason and Seeking Truth in the Sciences (1637). Found at https://www.earlymoderntexts.com/assets/pdfs/descartes1637.pdf, 19–20.

3. Some translations actually use "strings" instead of "voice."

4. Ps. 19:1–4.

5. Rom. 8:38–39.

6. Luke 5:17–26, KJV, italics added.

7. Jay Pathak and Dave Runyon, *The Art of Neighboring: Building Genuine Relationships Right Outside Your Door* (Grand Rapids: Baker, 2012).

8. Mark 12:31.

9. *Darius Goes West: The Roll of His Life*, Logan Smalley, director (Roll with Me Productions, 2007).

10. This concept of sin as the "impairment of relationship" is developed by Thomas Jay Oord in his highly accessible book, *Open and Relational Theology: An Introduction to Life-Changing Ideas* (Grasmere, ID: SacraSage Press, 2021), 108–9.

Chapter 7: "owh"   the salvation of god

1. John 1:14.

2. Matt. 16:26.

3. Luke 4:18–19.

4. Luke 4:21.

5. Matt. 5:44.

6. Matt. 5:39–41.

7. See Walter Wink's, *Violence and Nonviolence in South Africa: Jesus' Third Way* (Philadelphia: New Society Publishers, 1987).

8. See https://www.openhorizons.org/a-soul-with-size-bernard -loomer.

9. John 3:3.

10. Luke 3:22.

11. Luke 19:1-10.

12. See Will Campbell's memoir, *Brother to a Dragonfly* (1977, repr. Jackson: University Press of Mississippi, 2018).

Chapter 8: "poof"   the end, with god

1. For more on this, see John Polkinghorne, *Quarks, Chaos & Christianity* (New York: Crossroad, 1996), 90.

2. *Ferris Bueller's Day Off*, John Hughes, director (Los Angeles, CA: Paramount Pictures, 1986).

3. https://slate.com/technology/2014/03/asteroid-2003-qq47 -rumors-of-an-impact-in-march-2014-are-false.html.

4. Jer. 31.

5. Eph. 1:8–10.

6. See Kieran Setiya's book, *Midlife: A Philosophical Guide* (Princeton: Princeton University Press, 2017).

7. Alfred North Whitehead, *Process and Reality: An Essay in Cosmology*, rev. ed. (New York: Free Press, 1978), 525.

8. Rev. 21:5–6.

9. Luke 18:18–22.

10. Joel 2:28.

11. Mal. 2:6

12. Isa. 40:29–31.

13. Ezek. 36.

14. Luke 13:29–30.

15. Matt. 22:10.

16. Luke 14:18–24.

17. Matt. 25:10.

18. Matt. 25:31–46.

19. Rom. 8:39.

CPSIA information can be obtained
at www.ICGtesting.com
Printed in the USA
LVHW010237270723
753158LV00001B/1